THE DROP

THE DROP

HOW THE MOST ADDICTIVE SPORT CAN HELP US UNDERSTAND ADDICTION AND RECOVERY

Thad Ziolkowski

HARPER WAVE

An Imprint of HarperCollins*Publishers*

THE DROP. Copyright © 2021 by Thad Ziolkowski. All rights reserved. Printed in the United States of America. No part of this book may be used or reproduced in any manner whatsoever without written permission except in the case of brief quotations embodied in critical articles and reviews. For information, address HarperCollins Publishers, 195 Broadway, New York, NY 10007.

HarperCollins books may be purchased for educational, business, or sales promotional use. For information, please email the Special Markets Department at SPsales@harpercollins.com.

FIRST EDITION

Designed by Elina Cohen

Library of Congress Cataloging-in-Publication Data has been applied for.

ISBN 978-0-06-296593-6

21 22 23 24 25 LSC 10 9 8 7 6 5 4 3 2 1

For Juliana

Contents

Preface

Montclair, New Jersey

Late summer, early morning—warm, clear, windless. I load my sleepy twelve-year-old son and six-year-old daughter into the car, make final adjustments to the straps holding the longboard on the roof rack. Finding time to go can be complicated, but the way is simple: a straight shot on the Garden State Parkway, which flows downhill until it reaches the bridge across Raritan Bay. On the other side, a rest stop called Cheesequake then wetlands, stands of poplars, the occasional heron or osprey.

In Manasquan, there's a drawbridge over the estuary—lush green reeds and mudflats, sailboats at anchor, a glimpse of the inlet. The surf is small this morning, possibly flat, and I feel none of the haste that overtakes me when I know it's good or even pretty good—when I might put my wetsuit on backward or forget to apply sunblock or leave the lights on if I arrive at daybreak and return to find the car battery dead.

I get a parking spot near the inlet, which is a victory, and we're just early enough to avoid paying for beach passes. The waves I see as we crest the slight rise where the sand begins are indeed small but marvelously glassy and blue, shimmering in the morning sunlight.

Dropping our stuff—backpack and towels and sun-shielding tent and food—on the border between the surf and the swim zones, I feel the age-old urgency to "get amongst it," as the Aussies say. I smear sunblock on Teo and Gemma, then on myself, attach the boogie board leashes to their wrists, and watch them enter the water. As I'm scribbling wax on my board, two teenage lifeguards arrive and climb into their throne-like white chair. I attach the leash to my ankle and trot into the shallows, kicking through wavelets and crosshatching ripples. When the water is thigh-deep, I drop the board and place the fingers of my right hand on the deck in automatic fashion. Muscle memories, as of a first language.

I grew up surfing then quit it like a drug to focus on college. It was like throwing a psychic switch from body to mind—an old-fashioned, steampunk kind of switch that sparked and twitched and threatened to fly back the other way. When it finally did, surfing was no longer in the body position. In its place was drinking, then drugs. I was in New York City, the opposite of where I lived in my beachy provincial youth, but as in a dream surfing was at the end of the A subway line when I needed to find it again—Far Rockaway. It felt like falling to my knees, being taken back without question or reproach. I was given a kind of new body or an old reason to have a body, to be fit, to wake up early—to get sober.

Out in the lineup, I turn to check on Gemma and Teo. So

far, my carefully offhand and widely spaced invitations to climb on a board have been met with firm refusals. I understand. The ocean is scary and they are always encountering it anew, after weeks or months away. It's not important, I tell myself. It may even be for the best. I want them to experience surfing, to be conversant, but do I want them to become surfers? To be seized by it as I was? For school and most everything else to lose color and fade into the background? That's the risk—possession, addiction. And not only to surfing, if they had my proclivities.

I notice what appears to be a surf school gathering on the beach—pink and purple soft-top boards, a pink banner planted in the sand: GIRLS IN THE CURL. Before long, young girls accompanied by women instructors filter out into the lineup. The tide is dead low and their parents stand in the shallows taking videos with smartphones and shouting praise as the girls are pushed into waves, climb to their feet, and ride toward the beach with arms outspread like fledglings.

At the end of a ride, I notice Gemma watching them. She's left her boogie board on the beach. I nudge my board toward her. Wanna try?

Without taking her eyes off the surf-school girls, she nods as if in a trance and eases herself onto the deck of the board.

I walk us toward the lineup with Gemma lying prone, but the board is so boatlike for her that halfway out she stands up cheekily, showing off as we crest waves. On the backside of a bigger one, she windmills her arms and falls off, climbs back on the board laughing, stands up again. Having reached the lineup, I have her lie down toward the nose and I lie down behind her and paddle around, giving her a tour—over by the dark barnacle-encrusted jetty boulders, then back among the surfers waiting for waves. The surf zone is a dimension unto itself—the sunlight sparkling on the rolling, glassy blue water, the subtle sense of suspended or alternate temporality. Of being sleek and camouflaged like a dolphin and possessed of dolphin-like playfulness. There is nothing to be or become. Everything is all right, complete. This is the essence of what I wanted her and her brother to know—what I believe in enough to wish to bequeath or transmit.

A wave arrives and I swing around and paddle us into it, anchoring the back of the board and gripping the rails to keep it stable. Once we're shooting along in the whitewater, Gemma jumps to her feet without prompting and rides in a frozen crouch for a long dramatic stretch as I angle the board hard to the right. She's so small and the ride is going on for so long that the eyes of the Girls in the Curls parents and the rest of the beach have turned to follow us. Gemma seems to sense it: she dismounts at the end with a cannonball flourish.

"Again!" she says, and climbs back on the board. But now Teo, having witnessed his sister's glorious first wave, wants to try it, too, and waits impatiently in the shallows for her second ride, which amounts to a repeat of the first, to be over. I walk then paddle the much larger Teo out into the lineup, then into a wave; he gets to his feet and rides it for a good stretch, then falls off and immediately asks for another, eyes wide and excited. And so begins an endless round of their taking turns—two rides each—and squabbling over whether such and such a shorter or weaker wave actually counts as a turn.

By noon we're sun-scorched and famished. I set up the sun tent and we eat lunch huddled in its shade and afterward have an ice cream at Carlson's Corner, a take-out diner with umbrella-shaded tables. Gemma and Teo don't want to go home yet, but I insist we stay under the umbrella at our table until the fiercest heat and sunlight of the midday is past. They fetch their iPads from the car and settle in.

When we return to the beach later in the afternoon, everything is different. The sun has slipped behind a lid of clouds in the west, the beach is in shadow, and the crowds have thinned. The tide is peaking high rather than low, with foamy tongues licking at the sand near our towels, and a bigger, hectic, short-period wind swell has replaced the glassy morning waves. There's no sign of Girls in the Curl, the parents, the instructors, the girl students.

It's going to be altogether trickier to get beginner waves now and I stand surveying the situation.

"Are you coming?" Gemma asks at the edge of the shorebreak. "Let's go!"

Out of caution, I restrict us to the whitewater on the inside, but there's a trench just past the shorebreak and the rides are short-lived and disappointing, as Gemma is quick to let me know. "That doesn't count!" she shouts at Teo.

She turns to me. "That was *terrible*!" she scolds. She's very aware that people on the beach are watching her and can't abide disappointing her fans.

After another line of whitewater dribbles away in deep water before she can pop to her feet, she sighs with exasperation and points out to the lineup, where a few beginners bob around cluelessly. "Look at the *other* surfers, Daddy! Do what *they're* doing!"

This is too much. "All right," I say, patting the front of the board. She wants a real wave, we'll catch a real wave. "Get on."

I wait for a brief lull in the nearly incessant waves and sprint-paddle us past the inside bar untouched. We're just reaching the lineup when a set wave caps as we're cresting it at a steep angle and the whitewater sweeps Gemma backward, banging her head so hard against mine that I see a flash.

"Oh my God, are you okay?" I ask, rubbing my forehead and glancing at my fingers to check for blood. I'm expecting Gemma to tearfully insist on going in, but she surprises me by nodding gamely while rubbing the back of her head. "I'm okay. Let's go."

"Are you sure?"

"I'm sure!"

"Do you want to go in?"

"No, I'm fine!"

"Okay." I paddle us a bit farther out and we sit up to wait for a wave. The dark green water is alive with tossing, pushy swell energy. I'm uneasy now. That loss of control, my not having factored in how weak a hold Gemma would have on the board as we plowed through these bigger waves, has rattled me.

Looking back, I see the shore is much farther off than I expected it to be. I can barely make out Teo's head where he's hanging out in the shorebreak. Meanwhile, aside from a few lost-looking beginners, the lineup is empty. Gemma knows how to swim but not well and not in the ocean. I don't like how this scene is coming together, with that ominous unremarkable quality preceding terrible accidents.

The next wave that comes, I decide, we're catching it into the beach. And one arrives almost immediately, bigger than I would have preferred, but I turn and paddle for it.

"Okay," I say, "here we go!"

Instantly the wave seizes us and we shoot forward. Partially blinded by spray and sunlight, I see Gemma hop blithely to her feet then tumble straight into the drink as the nose buries itself in a chop. The board is an oldish, quite heavy nose-rider, ten feet four inches long. Underwater I grip the rails with all my strength as I'm spun like a riverboat paddlewheel, determined to keep it away from Gemma but fearful it might clip her anyway.

When I finally surface clinging to the board like a spar, I find Gemma dog-paddling in the bright fizzing foam nearby, wide-eyed and gasping.

It's shallow enough for me to stand. I reach out and sweep her gratefully up with one arm and set her on the board.

"Whoa!" I say, peering into her face. "Are you okay?"

She clasps my arm and gulps in air. When she's caught her breath enough to speak, she says, "Let's get another one!"

PART I

Liminality

Surfers are hardly unique. The allure of the ocean is enormous, mythic, virtually universal. Seeing it for the first time can have the force of a secular revelation. To swim or wade in it, or merely stand on shore and gaze, is entrancing, soothing, renewing. There is something enchanting about both the view of the vastness and the water itself, its texture and colors, the magic of its chemistry. The pulse of its life force is palpable and there is always a sense, however faint, of putting oneself invigoratingly at risk on entering it, of being tested, evaluated, scanned. Hence the costly annual pilgrimages of vacationers and dense clustering of populations along coastlines despite the exorbitant price of beach real estate and the rapidly increasing instability brought on by global warming.

But note that it's not out at sea, aboard a boat or a ship, that most people want to be—it's by and in it. The meeting of land and sea forms an elemental threshold with deep, primal resonance and magnetism. The land is like the awake rational mind of the present, the ocean the unconscious, irrational, archaic. The ocean shore is the geographic equivalent of dawn or dusk, of the transitional mode of consciousness between waking and sleep, an intermundial state in which the spirit is quietly loosened from its moorings and set adrift. Edges blur, identities become uncertain, shifting, subject to flux and transformation. New thoughts well up, changes of life direction are contemplated.

The term for interstitial places and states of consciousness is "liminal" (from Latin, *limen*, threshold), coined by early-twentieth-century folklorist Arnold van Gennep. The focus of van Gennep's hugely influential book is reflected in the title, *The Rites of Passage*, but he begins with a discussion of ancient borderlands between tribal territories. Often natural barriers such as marshes or forests, these zones are the original thresholds, their "magico-religious" properties arising in part from being neither here nor there, neither ours nor theirs. To enter a frontier or borderland is to pass into a new world, where one's status is uncertain and provisional. Though van Gennep doesn't mention the treacherous, ever-changing surf zone separating shore from open ocean, it, too, functions as a borderland and was until recently regarded as a realm of evil spirits, spiritual peril, and uncertainty in a variety of cultures—Indonesia, Africa, the Caribbean, even parts of Polynesia. Comparable beliefs also pervaded European coastal communities. The West rid the ocean of sea monsters beginning roughly with the Enlightenment, but even Westerners became aquatic en masse only within the past century or so.

Like entering a borderland, rites of passage and initiations strip away and suspend identities. Many such rituals, van Gennep noted, involve crossing an actual or symbolic threshold, hence the term "liminal." He divided these rites into three phases: the pre-liminal, in which individuals are separated from the group; the liminal or transitional itself; and the post-liminal or reincorporative, in which a girl, for example, having ritually become a woman, reenters the social group under the sign of this new identity and stature. Van Gennep extended the concept of liminality to include transitional states of place, situation, or time: moving from one house to another, or to a new city; starting college or a job, or graduating; New Year and birthday celebrations.

Addiction is liminal, too, an interstitial realm divided from workaday reality by an unseen veil. I think of the opioid addict lying, eyes closed in a nod, on flattened cardboard as rush-hour foot traffic troops past inches away. Even the functional addict, the executive or day laborer, lives in a dimension to one side of her nonaddict coworkers, isolated by preoccupation and dependence. Addicts—and surfers, too—are what Victor Turner, elaborating on van Gennep, calls "liminal personae," or threshold people, who exist on the margins of society in a state of social invisibility and lowliness.

Liminality crops up in neurobiological accounts of addiction: the reward system of the brain, which governs motivation and drive, is reshaped by sustained drug misuse, raising the "reward threshold" so that natural pleasures such as food and sex lose their interest and appeal. Only the drug of misuse stimulates the production of the levels of dopamine and other neurotransmitters enough to reach and crest the threshold, producing a high. The Tantalus-like tragedy of addiction is that the reward threshold grows ever higher until finally little to no effect aside from a feeling of relief from anxiety, discomfort, or misery is achievable.

Compulsive attempts to reach and cross the threshold end in overdoses, sometimes fatal, especially for opioid addicts.

Whatever causes addiction, whether trauma, genetic predisposition, social despair, sheer exposure and consumption, or some combination thereof, people who become addicts all seem to be haunted by an acute sense of lack or dislocation that has a liminal character—a being on the outside. Yet there is no reliable predictor, and whether this feeling of dislocation is distinct from one of generalized human-condition malaise or yearning remains inconclusive until it's too late and addiction actually arises.

To apply van Gennep's schema, the pre-liminal phase occurs with bingeing and intoxication. Once the high becomes preferable to the company of others, the addict disjoins from the initiatory group of casual users, taking a kind of secret vow of loyalty to the drug. With me it happened in the autumn of my second year of graduate school at Yale, where I was restless and poised to drop out. I was twenty-seven. In the background: my parents' divorce when I was eight, my stepfather's long unhappiness and suicide when I was seventeen, my younger brother Adam's mental illness that had landed him in Saint Elizabeth's psychiatric hospital and would lead to his suicide a few years later. I had broken up with one girlfriend by falling into bed with a new one. Walking together in the evening, the new girlfriend and I came to a dividing point between our neighborhoods. Did I want to come to her house? No, I was going to go home and write. At my apartment was a gram of cocaine, which I had just discovered was a wonder when it came to poetry and term papers, a guarantor of pure, all-nighter focus. I wanted nothing more than to be alone with this miraculous new muse, who asked nothing of me (yet) while making aesthetic objects of the anguish and confusion I felt about the breakup with my previous girlfriend and the broader predicament I found myself in, wavering on the threshold of the ivory tower.

THE LIMINAL PHASE proper is a realm of lost time, hidden excess, obsession, compulsion, shame, despair, physical and mental decline. Cocaine was like a person of enormous charm under whose spell I had fallen. When the honeymoon ended, I saw I had a problem and quit but eventually slipped into using again, always through drinking, which was a problem in its own right. Because it's never one thing only. I was also depressed, inconsolable in some root way, though there were to my mind so many good reasons to be depressed that it hardly occurred to me that it might be something more serious. When my friends left New Haven for the summer, I stayed behind out of inertia and found a job as a janitor. The white folding chairs being set out on the quad for graduation looked to me like headstones or the teeth of a gear. In August, I took an impulsive leave of absence and moved to the Lower East Side, where in certain bodegas cocaine was as easy to buy as cigarettes.

The post-liminal phase is marked by abstinence or death, in my case also by a return to surfing, at Rockaway Beach, which I now see acted as a rite of purification. Rehab is a kind of liminality preceding reincorporation into society, with 12-step or AA meetings functioning as intraliminal moments after abstinence and the addict's reentry into the workforce and family life. Yet the orthodoxy within the recovery community is that once an addict, always an addict, like the human who eats the food in the underworld. The liminality of addiction lingers and colors and stretches on into the future. I may attend the wedding yet from the raised glass of champagne I must not sip.

But having managed to quit, to be as cleanly and clearly on the other side as one can be, what then? Simply abstaining is unsustainable, we know. Neurologist David Zald articulates a consensus position among addiction researchers when he says that the key lies in identifying "a stronger alternative reward to overcome the compulsion to seek and engage in the addictive behavior." Graft onto the wound of liminality another and more salubrious piece of it: some combination of body work and spiritual practice, meditation and the "in the zone" trance brought about by intense exercise, ideally in wilderness—surfing, for instance.

The Hawaiian phrase *he'e nalu* expresses the essence: wave sliding. Bodysurfing was almost certainly the original form and remains the purest. Among Hawaiians there is an ecumenical tradition of riding all manner of craft—rafts, floats, outrigger canoes, stand-up paddleboards, bodyboards. New modes have appeared in recent decades: tow-in, kite, foiling. Another innovation is adaptive surfing, which focuses on designing boards to suit the needs of people with disabilities. It's all surfing, it's all legitimate, it will all work to immerse one in the curative surf-zone liminality—though not merely immerse: importantly for the recovering addict, surfing also offers the rush and thrill of catching and riding waves.

Though not a particularly dangerous sport, surfing puts the brain on high alert by dint of being conducted in the ocean, where the risk of death by drowning or injury, while statistically small, is nonetheless real and ever-present. The survival-obsessed brain responds by paying very close attention to everything in its perceptual field, with the result that self-talk and dark preoccupations are pushed to the periphery and quieted. It's this natural and irresistible concentration in the present moment that is one of the most powerful things about surfing for the recovering addict—silence, focus, a kind of chastened vigilance.

The neurochemical dividends are many: the aerobic demands of paddling out, usually through an obstacle course of whitewater, then catching and riding waves, flood the body with serotonin and endorphins, endogenous opioids that produce the famous "runner's high," along with improving the brain's ability to process emotions. The looming up of waves activates a fight-or-flight response that elicits adrenaline. The drama, thrills, and risks of wave riding proper call forth spurts of dopamine, the neurotransmitter of drive and wanting that plays a central role in habit formation, learning, and addiction.

All the while, there is the exalting natural beauty and multisensory richness of the ocean wilderness, the arena and medium of wave riding. The least bit of time spent in the wilderness stirs feelings of awe, which has its own neurochemical signature and has been found to countervail the destructive self-centricity of the addict. Awe inspires generosity, openness, and compassion.

Given the range and strength of these benefits, surfing would seem to offer a superb replacement therapy for recovering addicts. So let's go surfing. "It's simple," I overheard an instructor tell a beginner in the lineup. "Just look at the beach and stand up." But the instructor was doing the hard parts: selecting the waves and pushing the student into them at the right moment. Waves are what make surfing unlike other sports, even close relatives such as snowboarding, skateboarding, windsurfing, and hang gliding. A mountainside or paved surface is stable, after all. Even wind is a relatively continuous force. Shoaling ocean waves, on the other hand, are rapidly moving, morphing bands of liquid energy—looming like cobra hoods, shifting, lurching, abruptly receding as if stricken with stage fright. Waves have personality-like characteristics and being able to read them is the key to all, from discerning which ones are desirable to catch and catchable, to riding them well. As everyone discovers who gives it a try, surfing is for this reason dauntingly difficult, but its pleasures, which can be tasted from the first, are commensurate with that difficulty.

The classic arc is to begin as a child or teenager—until recently almost exclusively male and, on the mainland United States and in Australia, white—and spend many humbling if not humiliating months in a protracted rite of passage and liminality during which basic competency is acquired. Thus the "kook" becomes a bona fide surfer, able to catch and ride waves without being a danger to self or others and finding a submissive and silent place at the bottom of a local hierarchy composed of elders and betters. All surfers must undergo some version of this initiation, and the universality of the experience is the source of a sense of hard-won membership and recognition.

In recent decades an alternative path has been forged by adults—men, women, queer people, people of all races—

who are introduced to surfing in a class or on vacation or simply in imitation of surfers at their local beach. This is the group most recovering addicts will be a part of. Having fallen in love with surfing, these adult beginners can none-theless manage to surf only occasionally in the midst of juggling careers and family life. But no one is above the law: many, many hours in the ocean must be clocked in order to master the basics and acquire wave knowledge, with the result that this new class may never graduate, never quite emerge from a state of liminal lowliness. What's remarkable about this predicament is that it turns out not to matter. The self-confidence and openness that made them game to learn to surf to begin with permit this cohort to enjoy and savor the surfing they're able to do without being unduly self-conscious or burdened by where they may or may not stand in a hierarchy of technical ability, knowledge, and status. The pleasure and satisfaction taken by adult be-ginners amount to an implicit critique and rejection of the classic arc's stern paternalism and linearity, reasserting something that gets repressed by surfing's curious inter-nal conformism and self-policing: the radically personal nature of the sport, its irreverence for authority, even and perhaps especially authority wielded by surfers. By re-maining stuck in the middle phase of their rite of passage, adult beginners are compensated by what Victor Turner calls "communitas"—a spirit of comradeship and egalitar-ianism that springs up in the liminal state, when status and social rank have been stripped away and the power of the weak and humble prevails. Their good-humored, worldly presence in the lineup, along with the growing numbers of girls and women and people of color, has diversified and leavened the too often homogeneous, game-faced character of the sport.

Surfing in the company of others or with a friend may be necessary at first for reasons of safety and encouragement, but going out alone is best for the recovering addict, even if that means settling for inferior waves. Solitude reduces self-consciousness and performance anxiety and is most conducive to restorative inwardness. It's easiest to find the rhythm or pace of a swell alone, to take the right waves, and you will be most available for subtle, uncanny experiences that can aid in remaining sober.

One apparent irony or danger for recovering addicts when it comes to surfing as replacement therapy is that surfing has a pronounced addictive component of its own. Within the sport it's well known that it can often crab and parochialize the lives of its devotees. "It's sad to think of all the opportunities I missed because I'm so obsessively addicted to surfing," remarks big-wave rider Ken Bradshaw, who never had children, who restricted himself to one cocktail at dinner in order to be ready should the surf come up. "Don't be me. I don't have what most human beings want." Granted, Bradshaw is an extreme case, but most surfers can attest to ways in which surfing's hold on them has eaten into or tainted commonplace joys— Thanksgiving celebrations missed due to a great swell or miserably, twitchily endured for the same reason. If there's a difference between this subversion of everyday pleasure and what drug addiction does, it's not obvious. Like drugs, surfing attracts people inclined to zealotry and obsessiveness, then feeds and intensifies the tendency. Yet the very power and potential of surfing to become all-consuming actually argues for its adoption by recovering addicts— remember Zald's admonition to find a comparably potent substitute. And even if taking up surfing proves impossible or unsustainable, there are many things to be learned from it, transposed to other pursuits and passions.

Surfing is a kind of parable of addiction, but like other subcultures it's often understood crudely, through a few dated stereotypes or tropes. Accorded passing admiration for braving the waves as they trot down the beach, surfers largely vanish from the screen of collective awareness on entering the ocean, reappearing only rarely and for something exceptional, such as being attacked by a shark or towed into waves of record-setting size with Jet Ski assist. Meanwhile, despite taking place for the most part in plain view, surfing's typical acts and achievements remain curiously invisible, as if the liminality of the surf zone veils it from the eyes of noninitiates. I think back to the addict nodding on flattened cardboard amid rush-hour foot traffic—there and not there. Hardcore surfers like Bradshaw, surfers generally, fully qualify as members of Victor Turner's class of liminal personae. Crossing and recrossing the primordial threshold between land and sea, inhabiting an insular, self-contained dimension, surfers are liminal personae par excellence. Their invisibility springs from a kind of suspension. "They are at once no longer classified and not yet classified. Their condition is one of ambiguity and paradox, a confusion of all the customary categories." It's the betwixt-and-betweenness of threshold people like surfers and addicts that renders them invisible. They fall between the social cracks. The amphibiousness of surfers is consistent with this line of thought, their belonging both to land and sea and neither; as is a tendency toward gender fluidity in their appearance and the virtual nakedness of surfers, their having shed the social markers of clothing. According to Turner, nakedness has polyvalent meaning in liminality: it evokes both the nakedness of newborns and corpses, of life and death and neither life nor death. Symbolic nakedness is a signifier of the "sacred poverty" of monks and renunciates, and even though the nakedness of surfers is functional rather than symbolic, many are the social rewards renounced de facto in the course of a surfer's life.

One of the elements that has kept surfing on the margins is its vexed relationship to work. To be free to surf when the waves come up, surfers arrange to be underemployed, giving priority to the unpredictable behavior of the ocean rather than the time clock of wage-earning or salaried employment. "Don't get fired unless it's firing [i.e., unless the surf is excellent]," the motto of a surf forecasting website, succinctly conveys this cavalier attitude and its potential fallout. The phenomenon was noted with disapproval as early as 1820, when Calvinist missionary Hiram Bingham, freshly arrived on Oahu, was scandalized to see Hawaiians abandon their tasks, strip off what little clothing they wore, and dash to the ocean at the appearance of a good swell. But this was almost certainly a misrecognition. Hawaii at the time was still an intact archaic agrarian culture, with work and play interlocking so seamlessly with myth and ritual as not to properly exist, to be mistranslations. Priests at *heiaus* (altars) offered prayers for surf and flew kites to signal the arrival of good waves. There may well have been a component of fertility rite in the festive collective surfing Bingham witnessed: the god of fertility, Lono, was also the god of the sport and a surfer himself. Certainly part of what affronted the missionaries was the nudity and the sex that would take place at the shore around surfing. "The decline and discontinuance of the use of the surf-board, as civilization advances," Bingham later wrote, "may be accounted for by the increase in modesty, industry, or religion."

What came to pass in the twentieth century would doubtless have shocked Bingham: for it was religion and modesty of dress that fell into decline, surfing that flourished. Industry, however, did indeed increase and has dogged surfing ever since—while also accelerating its evolution. As it passed from an archaic agrarian society into an industrial one, surfing was shorn of its symbolic and ritual meanings—desacralized. A surfboard, for instance, was originally carved from a tree in the Hawaiian forest (with different species of trees being used for different sorts of boards). Before the tree was felled, a ritual offering of a fish was placed at the base of the trunk and prayers of gratitude intoned. Until the late 1950s, surfboards on the US mainland were also made from trees but the redwood or balsa was purchased from a lumberyard in anonymous planks, which were then glued together to form a blank. There was no spiritual connection or dimension: the lumberyard wood was regarded purely in terms of functionality and abandoned without hesitation when polyurethane foam was found to be a superior material.

In the industrial society where surfing was transplanted, the line between work and play was clear and absolute. Surfing fell neatly into the category of leisure activities such as tennis and fishing and baseball. As W. H. Auden said of poetry, surfing makes nothing happen—it is play in the highest sense, like dance with an element of toreador danger. But as Victor Turner observes, with the decrease in traditional rites of passage such as communion and bar mitzvahs and marriages, the sacred seeps into the realm of leisure and play, especially in collective forms such as rock concerts and mass sporting events—"liminoid," Turner calls leisure of this kind. Work has an arbitrary, obligatory character in industrial societies. That we play because we choose and want to, and that play often has seasons recalling the agrarian cycles of the preindustrial past, also increases its quotient of sacredness and liminality. In this roundabout process, surfing has been to a degree and in a new way resacralized, which helps make sense of the monkish devotion it inspires among initiates like Ken Bradshaw, along with the spiritual tone of testimonials by surfers, including this one. Turner approaches the question agnostically, as if there were, in any given social order, always a certain basic amount of what gets to count as sacredness. In the change from one kind of society to another, what is coded as sacred simply finds a new place in which to settle, like water. On the question of whether what is coded as sacred is truly sacred Turner and anthropology are silent. But surfers tend to be true believers.

The ocean shore is a threshold; a threshold is a crossroads. Gods of the crossroads are numerous—Osiris of ancient Egypt, Legba of West African vodun. In ancient Greece and Rome, it was Hermes, then Mercury. This species of god often has a trickster face or aspect, as if the uncertainties of such liminal places and states, the disorientation that comes with moving from one place or state to another, choosing between one road and another, make the temptations to deceive simply too great and numerous for a god to resist. What trick does the god of the surf-zone crossroads like to play? The trick of equivalence—to persuade that one kind of thrill, that of wave sliding, is the same as any other—the rush of drugs, for instance. *It's all good*, assures the trickster god: *one love!*

That many surfers have struggled with drug addiction will probably come as no surprise. Among top surfers a striking number have been addicts and even died of it, from Australian Kevin Brennan, who in the mid-1960s beat the best of that country's adult surfers in the nationals at the age of fifteen, then died of a heroin overdose when he was twenty-four, to Chas Chidester, who died of an overdose in 2018. People with addictive proclivities seem drawn to surfing for its physical and psychic demands, the intensity of its pleasures, the trancelike state that steals over one in the surf zone. But the era in which surfing's drug problem gained traction is that of the 1960s and 1970s, making it difficult to tease apart what belongs intrinsically to modern surfing from that of the youth culture it was a sun-bleached branch of. The liminality of surfing and that of addiction resonate, rhyme, and reinforce each other in many ways, some light, others dark.

When surfing spread outward from Hawaii in the early twentieth century, it came as if packaged with the easygoing hedonism of the "beachboys," Hawaiian surfers retained by Waikiki hotels to squire tourists out into the waves—an island lifestyle of hanging out, cooking freshly caught fish and shellfish, drinking, playing ukulele, and "talking story." But there was more to the beachboy phenomenon than giving surf lessons and letting the good times roll. The surf zone—*ka poʻina nalu* in Hawaiian—was one of the last realms where Native Hawaiians retained authority and rank due to their unmatched skill and ease in the ocean, and thus was (and remains) a space of cultural conservation, resistance, and reclamation.

In the nature-loving, newly aquatic California of the early twentieth century, the beachboy lifestyle was eagerly embraced along with surfing itself. Spirits, beer, and tobacco were the main intoxicants on the mainland, with amphetamines and pot occasionally finding their way into the mix. The hunter-gatherer self-sufficiency of the surf lifestyle—home brew and hooch, seafood stew cooked over open fires—saw the small Californian surf colonies through the Depression in style. This was the era of the term "surf bum"—a kind of double liminality, since the bum or hobo was already a threshold figure, tramping along the outskirts of the mainstream. But with the rising popularity of surfing and the crowding of lineups in the postwar period, especially after the boom following the appearance of the movie *Gidget* in 1959, the alcohol and excess fueled an occasionally violent territorialism with street-gang characteristics—Windansea versus Malibu. Meanwhile, beaches grew steadily more regulated and surveilled by the state. You were told by the town or city when and where you could surf. Lifeguard towers sprang up; bursts of shrill disciplinarian whistles floated over the waves.

It was in the mid-1960s that drugs came to suffuse surfing—a liminal era of enormous social upheaval and progress in civil rights, women's rights, gay rights, and the anti-war movement. Pot and hashish supplanted beer and booze as the mainstays, with a plethora of new drugs—psychedelics, cocaine, barbiturates, opium—leaching into beach towns. Because of its proximity to Southeast Asian sources, Australia saw heroin addiction rise among surfers. In both Australia and the United States, surfers were being drafted along with their nonsurfing peers, and the rampant experimentation with drugs is inseparable from the anxieties and nihilism generated by the war in Southeast Asia.

The impact of psychedelics on surf magazines and films is obvious beginning around 1967. A cinematic effect called "acid tracks" came into vogue—psychedelic color graphics flowing out from the tail of the board in radiating prismatic bands. In 1970, the height of the countercultural embrace of amphetamines, there was even a "meth model" board, advertised with the slogan "For Those Who Love Speed."

Surfers traveling the world in search of new and uncrowded breaks discovered that by doing a little smuggling—often secreting the hash, heroin, or cocaine inside compartments carved into their boards—they could extend their journeys and put off returning home to get a dreaded job or find an even more dreaded draft-board notification waiting. But the price for being caught was long jail sentences, sometimes in foreign lands—Thailand, Indonesia, Afghanistan—and the punishment for bumbling into territory controlled by the US gangs could be death.

As the number of surfers dead from ODs and the drug trade spiked in the '70s, the phrase "natural high" gained currency. The related embrace of health food diets, yoga, and various shades of Eastern spiritual practices must be seen against the same darkening backdrop. Another reaction was born-again Christianity, which claimed a number of converts among top surfers.

But when the liminal era of the 1960s and 1970s ended, the drugs kept coming, harder now, with no pretense of being agents of higher consciousness: cocaine was dominant in the 1980s, especially on the professional contest circuit. "Ice" (methamphetamine) arrived in Hawaii and Northern California in the 1990s, followed by pharmaceutical opioids in the 2000s.

There is a particular sadness and bitterness about the rampant addiction in Hawaii, the birthplace and mecca of surfing. As in Native American communities and huge swaths of the postindustrial Midwest and Appalachia, cultural disorientation and despair have rendered Hawaii vulnerable. Too many Native Hawaiians exist in a kind of internal exile. But the surf zone—*ka poʻina nalu*—remains a sphere of rightness and renewal, where the dispossessions that have transpired on land can be forgotten or seen afresh, through the prism of immemorial belonging.

The domination of other people, whose slow-motion defeat curses the world being wrested from them; the domination of nature, which replies to our instrumentalizing and mechanistic view of it by coming monstrously to life as vast wildfires and superstorms: addiction and the strands that compose it can often seem to have the same relentless and inescapable cascade.

Yet all manner of crisis, whether planetary or personal, create liminal zones as they push us to the brink. The brink is a threshold, a crossroads. What lies beyond, in the purest form of the liminal, is a time out of time, without attribute, history, or future—a realm in which any change can occur because none is necessary. Though there's no guarantee that paddling out any more than a walk in the woods will grant access.

What surfing does more reliably, as a practice, is re-awaken joy. The body, one's whole being, retains the thrill, remembers the sun that warms the earth, which makes the wind blow, which makes waves in the ocean. It's through the aperture of my connection to surfing that I feel and see and therefore believe in the world's magic and transfigura-tive power, its divinity.

Of the ways surfing has to hold one rapt, that its field of play is the ocean shore may be the most potent. In the mov-ing liminal water, renewal becomes possible. It's a matter of shedding or cleansing, as in a baptism. What is washed away? Encrusted self-conceptions, losses, gains, traits, traumas, attainments, and failures, resentments, carefully cultivated specialness and difference, self-pity, goals, re-grets, sins but also virtues: the grand illusion.

The Ballad of
Andy Irons

The greatest surfer ever to set foot on a board, Kelly Slater, born in 1972, grew up in Cocoa Beach, a scrappy, highway-bifurcated small city on the east coast of Florida. Slater's boyhood was rife with what addiction researchers call "adverse childhood experiences": a violent alcoholic father, a chaotic, embittering divorce, economic insecurity. According to this theory, the more "ace's" in one's childhood, the greater the likelihood of acquiring a serious addiction. Slater reacted by abstaining, tossing drugs and alcohol onto the sacrificial fire of his monstrous competitive drive. First the youngest world champ ever, at age twenty, then the oldest, at thirty-nine, Slater has won eleven world championships, crushing the dreams of entire generations of contenders under his heel in the process and still competing on the world tour, where he remains a perennial threat to claim yet another title as he nears the grandfatherly age of fifty. The King, he's called, and the GOAT ("greatest of all time").

There was, however, one young knight able to dethrone the King in his prime, to bring the GOAT to tears of anguish and frustration—Andy Irons, or AI. Six years Slater's junior, Irons emerged as a challenger at the midpoint of Slater's reign. There was by then a longstanding resentment of Slater's suffocating dominance, a weariness with the ubiquity of his image in the press and films and videos. In addition to freakish flexibility and a gymnast's springy strength, Slater was blessed with matinee-idol good looks. He dated Pamela Anderson, hung out with rockers. His lone misstep was taking a year off from the professional tour to act in the abysmal TV melodrama *Baywatch*. The sheer bottomlessness of his hunger to compete and win, to be declared the best, could seem vaguely obscene or pathological within surfing, which has always had a conflicted relationship to official competition and mainstream fame that Slater was importing. His willingness to play mind games with competitors was another blemish. But on the whole, given how starkly superior he was in the surf, he wore his transcendent success and wealth with remarkable grace and charm, even humility, when it might so easily have been otherwise. He was, in short, too good, slightly sanitized, unreal, and white bread. He even wore a white wetsuit. The sole consolation for Slater haters was that the King was rapidly going bald.

Andy, by contrast, was a shaggy-haired, hard-partying, Metallica-loving throwback to the hedonistic 1980s, emotionally hot and spontaneous where Slater was smolderingly cool and strategic. Irons snatched the crown from Slater not once but three years in a row, from 2002 to 2004. Thanks to the Slater-Irons rivalry, professional surfing, forever in doubt both as a gauge of excellence and as entertainment, actually worked as spectacle. People in the non-surfing world paid attention and Irons joined Slater in the global sports pantheon.

I happened to see Andy just after he won his first world title, in December 2002. He was standing in the road on Kauai, board under his arm, chatting with someone in a pickup. He looked like a god: tall, perfectly proportioned, wet hair swept back on a handsome head. Lazily I ascribed his triumph simply to having grown up on this wave-rich, breathtakingly beautiful island—to having been blessed to a fault. But Andy had his adverse childhood experiences, too, I found out later: the dyslexia that tracked him into special education classes, which he was teased about endlessly and led him to conclude that he was stupid; the divorce of his parents when he was eleven; simply growing up a haole boy in Kauai might have amounted to an extended adverse childhood experience. Laird Hamilton, who attended public school on Kauai after his surf-star stepfather, Billy Hamilton, moved the family there in 1971, says about the experience: "Every day I was tested: fights, scrapes, always gettin' messed with. Slapped in the back of the head. You're reading your book in math class and a guy comes up from behind and rams your face into the desk. Then you gotta get up and brawl with him, then you both get suspended. That was the rule, some kind of fight or harassment daily."

On top of all these challenges, Andy was diagnosed at nineteen with bipolar disorder following a psychotic break he had after losing in the early rounds of his first contest on the world championship tour. He was prescribed medication but soon quit taking it because he disliked the effect.

Like many people with bipolar disorder, Andy treated his condition with recreational drugs. But he also had surfing. "The ocean balanced out his chemical imbalance," his younger brother, Bruce Irons, remarks in the documentary *Andy Irons: Kissed by God*.

It was when Andy defeated him in the final seconds of the 2003 Pipeline Masters that Slater wept. Winning would have given Slater the world championship, which he planned to dedicate to his father, who had died of cancer the year before. He stood, head bowed, under the spray of an outdoor shower and sobbed.

But the fever-pitch intensity required to best the King proved unsustainable. Andy came in second to Slater in 2005 and 2006. After the addictive rush of winning outright, runner-up had the force of a rip-off. The spontaneity that dazzled in the surf took the form of temper tantrums on the beach. Andy got into fistfights, broke his board in a rage. The power we idolize in champions looks godly on the field but dangerous and ugly run amok.

By 2007 Andy's "partying" had flared into full-blown addiction, chiefly to OxyContin, which he mixed with coke or meth or other drugs. He carried around a pill grinder, a bottle of 80-milligram OxyContins, and an ounce of coke. Andy's main sponsor, the Australian surf apparel brand Billabong, could no longer ignore the problem. It was July. Andy had just won a competition in Chile while blasted on coke and pills. At the urging of his father on Kauai, a Billabong rep met Andy at the airport in Los Angeles and told him in effect that this was an intervention: it was time to enter rehab. Andy went peacefully. The main sponsor is everything for a pro—not only the bulk of income but legitimacy in the watchful, status-conscious eyes of the surf world. Andy knew that Billabong, which paid him a reported $650,000 per year, was poised to drop him if he didn't at least try to get clean. But Billabong needed Andy, too: he was their primary brand ambassador, the one whose image graced the covers of their sales brochures, festooned the walls of their retail outlets. To let Andy flame out, or, worse, taint the brand with scandal, would be very bad for business.

Andy was driven directly from LAX to Promises, the posh rehab facility in Malibu, where he spent just ten days then left to compete in a world tour event in South Africa. Billabong arranged for him to room with a sober "minder" but at the end of the contest, rather than return to Promises to complete the program, Andy assured Billabong that he was fine now.

And he was for a few months, but in November 2007, while celebrating his marriage to Lyndie Dupuis, he relapsed and Billabong again insisted he return to Promises. This time he completed the program and came out feeling that he had truly come to terms with his addiction. He even let it be known that he planned to go public about his struggles but in the end decided against it.

With Billabong's encouragement, Andy took a leave from the world tour for the 2009 season. He was deeply burned out and ready to quit, but professional surfer was the only identity he had ever had. Who was he otherwise? No one, nothing. He slipped into an opioid-fueled depression that lasted for two months, then pulled out of it and went with Lyndie to live in a house rented by Billabong in Australia, where he trained hard, surfing every day, and stayed clean, which was easier there: opioids had yet to take hold in Australia.

In 2010, his comeback year, he set himself the goal of winning one more world tour event—no small feat even for Andy, especially after a three-year slump. He was eliminated in the early rounds in February in Australia, then surfed better in Brazil in April. In June, in Fiji, Andy had the best waves but started or tried to start a fistfight with another surfer over drugs, which got so out of control that he had to be restrained by a former navy SEAL and a cage fighter and then sedated. Billabong imposed a hefty fine. But in September Andy did it, taking first place at Teahupoʻo, the lethal reef pass where he won the first contest ever held there when he was only eighteen. He had long worried unaccountably about being perceived as a kook for failing to sustain his early level of competitive intensity and success. With the win at Teahupoʻo, he felt he could now honorably retire and devote himself to being a good husband to long-suffering Lyndie and a doting father to their son, who was due to be born in a month. He could deepen his involvement in organizing surf contests for Kauai youth, which he and his brother had taken up. He could even go public about his drug problem and make a real impact on the surf world and beyond.

Or he could die.

In October Andy flew reluctantly from Oahu to Puerto Rico to compete in a world tour event. He was having chest pains beforehand, and after being examined by a doctor he was told to go for testing when he returned to Hawaii. He had also relapsed again and was trying to wean himself off opioids ahead of the contest but wound up going through withdrawal on the flight there. He arrived so disheveled and red-eyed that he was told not to stay at a trade show where he was autographing posters. He missed his first heat, claiming to be sick with the flu, then withdrew from the contest altogether and caught a flight out. At a layover in Miami he bought coke from a friend and partied. He caught a late flight out of Miami and was en route back home to Hawaii when he was found dead in a Dallas airport hotel room. The covers were pulled up to his chin. Slater clinched his tenth world championship the day after the news broke.

The family put out a statement suggesting that Andy died of dengue fever, which was met with widespread skepticism. His reputation for partying was too well established, the dengue fever story too bizarre. With the international press clamoring to know the truth, Andy's inner circle refused to say more, which became the secondary story for some time: the surf world's tribal closure in the face of a global media onslaught, the unwillingness to pay the full price of fame versus the family's right to grieve in peace and avoid divulging what they deemed to be private matters if they so chose. The family was dealing not only with the stigma of drug addiction but specifically its appearance of monstrous selfishness: how could Andy have been so selfish as to overdose when he had a wife who was eight months pregnant with their first child? Aware that the autopsy might show traces of drugs in Andy's system and confirm the world's leering presumption, the family hired lawyers to delay its release.

There is a strong pull, when someone young dies unexpectedly, to believe that it can't be true or real, that he might yet walk through the door despite everything. This desperate impulse to suspend time, to leave open the door for a miracle, may have played a part in the family's decision to postpone release of the coroner's report: if the official word does not become known, the death is not completely real and final.

Andy had died once before, after all. It was at the end of a boat trip in Indonesia, on his twenty-first birthday. He got drunk and did a line of what he thought was coke but turned out to be morphine. Having passed out, he soon stopped breathing, and turned blue. Someone fetched Art Brewer, the surf photographer and de facto chaperone of the trip. Using CPR, a surfer got Andy breathing but he stopped again and turned blue, so Brewer and the others loaded him into a car and raced to a hospital, where Andy was given oxygen but flatlined repeatedly. They then took him to what they mistakenly thought was a hospital with an intensive care unit, then on to a third, which did have one. He flatlined for some minutes and had to be brought back with paddles. One of his lungs collapsed and was rein-flated. He slipped into a coma again. Through this endless night Brewer sat anxiously by the bed. He was old friends with Andy's parents and imagined calling to tell them their son had died on his watch. It was six hours before Andy finally opened his eyes.

In *Andy Irons: Kissed by God*, Bruce recalled the time Andy talked about this episode. The brothers were alone together in a room following the 2007 contest in Chile, the one Andy won while high on coke and pills. They were drinking and doing drugs. "Are you afraid of dying?" Andy asked, apropos of nothing.

"Yeah," Bruce admitted, "I'm afraid of dying."

"Well, brother, there's nothing to be afraid about. Remember when I died in Indo, and I was on that table, dead, for like eight minutes? I was out of my body and on the other side. It's all real—the light, the tunnel. I was in this other place and it was real nice and comfortable and warm. And when I was looking down at my dead body, I didn't like how I felt in that world, how I felt in that body. I didn't want to go back."

When the autopsy report was finally released in May 2011, it gave the world its drug story and the family and Billabong what they sought: a measure of cover. The medical examiner found a pharmacopeia in Andy's bloodstream—Xanax, Ambien, marijuana, methamphetamine, methadone, alcohol, and cocaine—but ruled that the main cause of death was a severely blocked heart artery: "The primary and the underlying cause of death is ischemic heart disease."

Billabong renamed the Pipeline Masters the Billabong Pipe Masters in Memory of Andy Irons and created an AI Forever line of beach apparel—board shorts, T-shirts, trucker hats.

A paddle circle memorial is a ceremony invented or perhaps revived by the beachboys in Waikiki in the early twentieth century. Surfers gather on shore then paddle out to the lineup or just past it, where they join hands in a circle. A brief eulogy is given, then the ashes, if present, are poured into the water and attendees throw flowers and leis into the circle, splashing water upward and shouting. There were famous ones for Duke Kahanamoku in 1968 and Eddie Aikau in 1978.

The first paddle circle for Andy was held at the competition he had withdrawn from in Puerto Rico, which was suspended when news of his death reached them. Later in November there were others convened in Huntington Beach, Bali, Australia, Brazil, France, Italy, Spain, Virginia, and Florida.

The one at Pine Trees on Kauai, the beach where he grew up surfing, was held close enough to shore that at the appointed hour some people simply swam out. I wasn't there; I watched videos of it later. Most people wore leis. There were kayaks, stand-up paddleboards, bodyboards, outrigger canoes, small boats. A water patrol Jet Ski flew a Hawaiian flag that had "AI" spray-painted on it in black letters like graffiti, another ski flew the handsome Kanaka Maoli, said to have been King Kamehameha's flag. Mostly there were people on surfboards, more than a thousand by the time the ceremony began—the largest paddle circle anyone could remember.

At the center, in a boat with a blue tarp roof, were Andy's mother, father, brother, and wife. A tree with hearts at the tips of its branches and the word "Andy" enclosed by a heart had been painted in red on Lyndie's bare pregnant belly.

Over a loudspeaker, a woman kahuna said prayers and blessings in Hawaiian then in English. When the kahuna concluded her blessing, everyone whistled and shouted and splashed the water. Leis made of ti leaves and plumeria blossoms were laid on the surface. A helicopter swooped in and hovered, raining flower petals down. Each member of the family leaned in turn over the side of the boat and tipped a portion of Andy's ashes into the ocean. Their raw, racking grief, especially that of the wife and the brother, was almost unbearable to witness. Searing fragments of memories and emotion welled up within me, of the death of my own brother and the years surrounding it.

People sat in silence for a moment then turned and began swimming and paddling in, returning to shore, to life on earth. A number of them caught and rode waves. The helicopter flew off. From above, the surfboards looked like scattered feathers.

Biophilia

My parents split up in 1968, when the laws regulating divorce were liberalized. Proof of "cruelty" or "marital infidelity" was no longer necessary: a simple claim of "irreconcilable differences" sufficed. They had married when they were just out of their teens and were still in their twenties. For them, the break was years in the making or unmaking, something they saw from afar and gradually came to accept as inescapable, though also promising new possibilities, new life.

For me, it was like a sudden downpour that caught me in a kind of boyhood paradise—exploring the woods in the company of my father, swimming in the Gulf of Mexico, drawing. My first memory and emblem of this prelapsarian era is a blue minnow in a jar of water on the windowsill of my bedroom. My father had trapped it in the creek behind our house in Chapel Hill using a funnel of screen. It was early morning. I gazed at the tiny wondrous fish and it gazed back at me. But the creek was polluted and through a paper cut my father contracted blood poisoning. Red streaks appeared on the inside of his forearm—unexpected and evil, like an undertow that might bear him off.

The divorce a few years later was that undertow. I turned and my father was gone. A new man began arriving in the evenings to take my mother out on dates: Pat. He was drunk the first time they met, his car so dented and dinged it looked like it had been in a crash derby. If he wanted to be with her, he would have to quit, my mother told him early on. And he did—until the final months, eight years later.

My mother took a job and after school my brother and I went to the house of a harried woman who looked after kids like us, most of them younger and snot-nosed. This was in the suburbs of northern Virginia, where we had moved following my parents' separation. The house reeked of boiled hot dogs and soiled diapers and I slipped away to the park across the street when I could.

Which is where I find myself as I think back, alone on a bench in the late fall. I'm staring bleakly at the colorless park, at the dull brick houses around it. And my mood is a new one: despair cut with grief and anger.

Then came more news: Pat would be joining our family as stepfather, though not, my mother hastily added, until we moved to the east coast of Florida, where he had landed a job. Florida! Much as I disliked and distrusted this new man, he was the conduit to something almost unutterably wonderful—living by the ocean in Florida.

On the way there, my brother and I stayed for several months with our maternal grandparents in Alabama. Then in Florida we lived first in an apartment in Indian Harbour Beach, later in a rental near Sebastian Inlet, and finally in a house on Andrews Drive in Melbourne Beach. But these were never quite our homes either—they were Pat's. Ever since this time I have felt like a guest of others, other families, other clans, subtly peripheral, provisional, petitioning.

I felt at home in the ocean, however, which drew me to it as the woods had. Why? The theory that comes closest to a satisfying explanation is that of biophilia: we are most alive and at ease in the wilderness and among the myriad other species teeming there, because ocean and forest and mountain are where our ancestors spent the vast preponderance of evolutionary time—three million years versus the very recent historical past of the agrarian era. Cities, towns, suburbs, and, by extension, digital spaces deprive us of this birthright, and in its absence arise the spiritual and psychological ills characteristic of modern life.

A related idea, sometimes called "blue mind," has it that to be near or in a body of water—stream, lake, ocean, even swimming pool—induces a pleasant, meditative state. Again, as a consequence of ancestral life, in this case of our having been so preoccupied with finding sources of water that simply to be in water's presence soothes and reassures, allowing our thoughts to drift, to turn to matters other than whether we have enough to drink and thus to survive: water and meditation are wedded forever, as Ishmael observes in *Moby-Dick*.

Surfing in 1970 was associated with long-haired delinquency, drugs and drug running, draft dodging, a general sketchiness. There was no professional tour to lend the sport a patina of legitimacy, no classes or camps or doting parents watching from the beach, no surf families smiling intergenerationally upon one another in the lineups, and nary a girl or woman or anyone above the age of twenty-five. Lifeguards were the exception to mile after mile of empty beach.

For my tenth birthday my mother bought me a used Surfboards Hawaii longboard—just left on the scrap heap of surf history by the collective switch to shortboards—and I carried it to the beach alone, placed it in the shorebreak, and paddled. There were no leashes. When I fell—and I did little else at first—I swam for the board, which was usually on its way to the beach, though sometimes, having hit me on the head, floating nearby. The ocean was a realm not of tranquility or love but rough justice, indifference that could feel like stern acceptance, a hiding in plain sight.

Like a refugee, I felt I could not go back, that I had to make this work. When the ocean glare gave me a case of snow blindness—bloodshot, wincingly hypersensitive eyes—I strapped on a pair of sunglasses using rubber bands and paddled out. A stray board opened up a wound on my scalp that sent me to the emergency room; I was back in the water the day the stitches were removed.

As for the citizens whose ways I observed so closely, I was either ignored by them or sneered at and threatened. They comported themselves like natives, but when they finally took me in, I discovered they were like me—lost boys.

The intensity of what I'm feeling as I learn to surf—excitement, fear, ecstasy, panic, triumph, humiliation—activates certain neurons and causes them to pass potent neurochemicals to others. The looming up of a wave, big or small, triggers my ten-year-old limbic center, whose function is to answer the question: Approach or flee? The brilliant thing about surfing is that it splits the difference between fight and flight: one turns and paddles away from a wave-beast, but this flight is a way to catch it, like running alongside a wild horse in order to leap onto its back. New synaptic connections ramify and recombine, like rivulets of rain on a windshield or lightning, while others slip into disuse, go dark, die out. There is no ethics in this autonomic, reticular world, no concepts of good or bad governing how or whether synaptic networks come into being to make swifter and reflexive my response to surfing, which ones flicker out through neglect. "What fires together wires together" is the promiscuous law of neuroplasticity—that is, cells active in the same instance tend to link up and collaborate, an interrelationship is solidified—"wired"—by repetition. Still, there are certain kinds of experience that have more power to alter the brain's synaptic networks than others. Novel, deeply engaging encounters, especially where learning is involved, sculpt with the greatest authority, scope, and depth. At no time in the course of life does more change take place than in childhood and adolescence, when learning is occurring in huge gulps. The synaptic formations established during this time, which underwrite habits of body and mind, also seem to be the most lasting and difficult to undo, to reshape. The first cut is the deepest.

It's like—and may be—epigenesis, a revision of my natal code. After my first time surfing, "I" am not purely, humanistically deciding (or ever really was in this view) whether I would like to go surfing again: the powerful initial experience has sparked cascades of synaptic reordering that predispose me to hoist the heavy board that nearly knocked me out and carry it back to the beach for more. I am now neurochemically biased in favor of surfing, with each subsequent encounter further strengthening and entrenching the rewiring initiated by the first time, and so on in a feedback loop in which the "surfing" configuration and its host of cues gets privileged over other things, such as drawing and museum-going, pastimes I enjoyed as a city boy but that now seem decidedly wan and dull.

ROUGHLY ONE IN four of my friends were fellow children of "broken homes," a sappy phrase we never used except derisively. The broader reaction of the culture to the rampant divorce rates was one of naturalizing and neutralizing and we fell into line, adopting a blasé posture toward our complicated lot, the stepparents and stepsiblings, the jet travel to far-flung fathers during vacations. But we were the survivors of a major upheaval: the columns broken during this period would never be repaired. We came away knowing something intact families were innocent of: it can all fall apart.

In other ways, we knew little. A fog of war hung in the air. My mother steadily represented the status quo—the divorce and her remarriage, the vast distance separating my father and me—as something settled and amicable, civilized and for the best. Years later I learned that when the final moving out was taking place, my father and Pat had come close to blows. And reading my parents' correspondence, I was surprised by the bickering that went on behind the scenes, mainly objections raised by my father, a professor of classics, about the amount of child support he was being asked to send, and steely itemizing of the costs by my mother. But she did not criticize or diminish my father in my presence. His periodic phone calls were announced with respect and my annual visits to Washington, usually in August, were sacrosanct. There was nothing wrong, nothing to grieve, no real loss.

I drank deeply from this cup. It was like my first drug experience, though as with any drug it had side effects and lost power over time. It wasn't simply the emotional violence of the divorce I was suffering in the wake of. On a dim, occult level, I believed that the move to Florida had been underwritten by it, my father exchanged or sacrificed for this miraculous, sun-drenched existence. On a still deeper level, I felt anguish and confusion about having failed to be what I had always assumed I was: the product and embodiment of the magic that had attracted my parents to each other and should by all rights have kept them together.

I thought of my father as exiled, but I was the one living in a frontier world. Alligators lay in the drainage ditches, vast tracts of impenetrable palmetto scrub bordered the playing fields and neighborhoods. People had names like Pittman, Sojourner, McAllister, Mead—settler names that tripped off the tongue of a teacher or coach reading down a roster. In my father's absence, in the absence of a college town where it might have had some authority, our name was just a stumbling block, an invitation to tell a Polish joke. Shamefacedly I proposed taking my stepfather's name, but in this Pat was wise and gently refused.

Though far away, my father emitted a signal, barely detectable over the crashing of the waves in the early years of my obsession with surfing but one I homed in on as I grew more bookish and serious about my studies. There was a kind of exchange program that allowed the child of a professor at one school to attend for free the school of another. Perhaps I could go to college where the waves were good, like the University of Hawaii, my father suggested. He didn't dare presume that I would alter my trajectory to include or suit him. He had reacted to the divorce by detaching himself, hoping for the best but from the safe remove of an avuncular admirer or family friend. He was resigned to getting the occasional postcard from his gone-native surfer son with the sun-bleached hair and puka-shell necklace. When in the end I decided to go to the university where he taught and live in his house, it surprised and touched him. I was going to "get to know my father again," I liked to tell people.

But I had never really ceased knowing him. What I secretly hoped was that we would become father and son again, and what I discovered was that the space a father would have occupied within me had closed up.

IN THE BACK of a drawer I come across a small blue plastic case containing a dozen or so slides. I remember them vaguely. They were taken in Florida with a 35-millimeter camera I later used in photography class. I keep meaning to send them to my younger brother Jason, who was their main occasion—our mother pregnant with him, his infancy—the honeymoon years.

I pick one from the stack and hold it up to the light. It's a close-up of my stepfather lying bare-chested on his back on the beach. Stretching his arms, he's turned toward the camera wearing an intimate, gratified expression.

Across the decades, through the layers of affection and even love I came to feel for the man, the image sends an unpleasant shock down into my core. His sheer initial presence, deepened by the otherness of his dark hair and skin and eyes, was a violence I experienced in a kind of gagged silence, forbidden by an array of forces to acknowledge or express my outrage. I have to resist an impulse to look away, to break the current between his eyes and mine.

The enigma and tragedy of Pat. He had won my mother and had a beautiful son with her. He was living in Florida, where he could fish and play tennis year-round, as he had long dreamed of doing. His two children from his first marriage lived across the peninsula and visited easily and often.

It was not enough. Or did not address or mend some obscure psychic fracture. Or silence the fatal judgment being rendered by an inner voice—the voice of his father, according to my mother. A big athletic man, he could be buoyant and playful, but his characteristic mood was touchy, irritable, brooding. When he lost his temper, the threat of violence was ever-present within the buffeting shouts, the chopping gesture of a hand, an abrupt stalking away in disgust followed by an equally abrupt return and resumption of the tirade. One sat very still, expression carefully blank, and waited for the storm to pass. I thought of my parents' divorce as the price of admission to paradise and surfing but in fact it was Pat and I paid it daily. We all did. Pat paid Pat.

This photo of him on the beach is from the first few months, before Jason was born, before it became clear that living in the Garden with his Eve would not suffice, hence before the full reality of the man had come forth into the light. The trust and respect that grew up between us, the compassion I could feel for him, softened and blurred the original force of his entry into my world in retrospect. But my psyche took a picture and it may as well have been this one: a stranger in the place once occupied by my father.

NOW I PICK another slide from the blue case. Holding it up to the light, I see myself at my surf rattiest: hair white-blond and shoulder-length, face and skinny bare torso baked brown, nose peeling. I'm seated in a wicker chair holding an infant Jason, which puts my age at eleven, summer or early fall of 1971.

It's a moment I remember clearly and in a way prefer to all others. I'm myself but still childlike, androgynous, not yet distracted by sexual desire and the grim vow to somehow "make a mark" that would isolate me and drain the color from things. The world consists of the town and the beach and teems with mystery and power, like a rain forest. I have a twin-fin that is coaxing me into trying new maneuvers—hooking sideways at the top of a wave where the crest can shelter me like a wing; nose riding. I've begun to win the notice of the dozen or so high-schoolers who dominate the local break and form a realm or tribe unto themselves, with its own lore and dialect and style. Even their unofficial leader, Johnny, with his head of tight Apollonian curls and uncanny surfing, has deigned to acknowledge me. All is promise and potential, flashes of light in the cloud of unknowing.

But in the eyes of what counts as polite society—the engineers drawn to the area by NASA, military families attached to Patrick Air Force Base, a thin layer of moneyed WASP elite—I'm trash: dark-skinned, long-haired, bare-foot, and shirtless, without membership in church or club. The rejection comes first from them, but I suppress this and persuade myself that it's the other way around and I find them contemptible—pasty, conformist, gutless. Whose view of the town is better than a surfer's, whose joy greater when the waves are good and school is ditched? I alchemize their disapproval into the liqueur of the rebel, the ambrosia of the beautiful loser.

One day, having surfed all afternoon, I walk up the beach to the crest of the bluff and step over a low wooden fence whose top plank has been kicked away for ease of trespass. We cross this lot so often a path snakes between the trunks of the feathery evergreens everyone calls Australian pines, which filter the sunlight and shed needles that lie in drifts on the sandy ground. Seated in a circle off to one side of the path are a dozen or so teens, some familiar at a glance, others unknown. A whiff of pot reaches me and following a whispered exchange my name is called.

I lean my board against the trunk of a tree and approach as if summoned to receive an honor. A pretty girl smiles approvingly and pats the ground beside her. I'm a kind of pagan pet or mascot, living proof that the pot-smoking youth are winning the generational struggle. Which is ironic, since for me it's been more ordeal than pleasure, pot smoking, darkened by thoughts of its illegality and the problem of avoiding detection by my sharp-eyed and worldly mother and stepfather. The whole project of getting high seems doomed to be exposed and punished.

But maybe this time it will be different and I will know the bliss or at least the amusement the others are on such familiar terms with. The main thing is that I've been included, called by name. I'm really no different from the kind of kid who joins a gang, which is to say a family to replace the one that broke apart.

One of the high-schooler clique is master of ceremonies. Tall and clownish and telling stories as he rolls, he sends joint after joint around the circle as if intent on smoking us into oblivion. When I finally rise to go some indeterminate time later, I can barely feel my body or use my mind. Like a slain man I pick up my board and walk along the path in the near dark, climb over the low fence along the road, disentangle my bike from the others left there in a heap.

Cars stream past, headlights on in the dusk. The sound is like a voice growing angrily louder that then batters me and dies away. This will never end, there will never be a break in this demonic stream, then somehow I'm across to the other side and trotting down the street.

In the quiet, I become aware of my heart. It's beating too hard, too fast. I stand still and listen inward. I'm having—it's suddenly clear—a heart attack.

At which point Johnny materializes on the air like the god he is to me.

What's happening? he asks, peering at me.

I smoked with Steve and them. And my heart—

I'm listening inward again, one hand pressed to my chest.

Your heart?

It's beating too fast—too fast, Johnny!

How much did you smoke?

A lot.

How much is a lot?

I need to go home. I need to tell them. I could die, Johnny.

Johnny shakes his head. I got a better idea.

What?

He motions with the board he's holding. Come surfing.

It's nighttime, Johnny.

There's a full moon.

He points, but I'm listening inward again.

But my heart—

Your heart's gonna be fine. Come.

I hesitate then fall into step with him. We cross the high-way, climb the fence in the dark beneath the trees. The circle is still seated off to one side of the path, coals moving.

Beyond the gloom, something vast is shining. I step over the broken fence and see it.

The ocean is lit to the horizon by moonlight. I move down the sand. Velvety black shadows fill the divots and footprints, and skittering presences appear at the edges of my vision—ghost crabs.

A tongue of foam licks my feet. Johnny trots past and into the shorebreak. I listen down into myself, but over the din of the surf my heart is inaudible. I wade into the warm shorepound, drop the board, and paddle.

As in a dream or a surfing hereafter, the whole clique is out, calling one another into the waves, hooting. As I sit with them in the lineup, a wave comes to me alone and I'm up and riding in extreme slow motion. Each ridge and contour of the face passes into the board and up through my legs like an intricate signal I obey without thought.

As I reach the shoulder, I see Johnny and someone else watching as they paddle over. His white teeth as he grins.

And I know then I'm not going to die, that I'm coming down.

FOLLOWING THAT NIGHT and most of the way through adolescence, I led a relatively wary, abstemious life, resolutely declining offers of pot and scarier psychoactives like mushrooms. Meanwhile, my peers were trying these things for the first time, with some becoming daily users.

I think of a boy I'll call Rusty, who had an even earlier introduction to pot than I did but apparently nothing comparable to frighten him off. By the time he was thirteen, his infectiously sunny affect had clouded over, his default expression became a low-lidded gaze into the near distance. I was troubled by it but also felt a curious—and in retrospect telltale—envy: Rusty was undivided by other allegiances—to football and baseball and a girlfriend, as I was by then. Rusty smoked pot and he surfed; he surfed and he smoked pot. He had found a kind of sacrament, a daily bread. He was like what I imagined a Rasta to be— aloof, devout, unalterable.

My younger brother, Adam, started smoking pot not long after I did, at eight or nine, doubtless in imitation of me, though he didn't follow my lead when I abruptly quit, and he would in all likelihood have kept at it but for the undeceivable Pat. The decisive moment came when Adam failed to show up for a Little League game. Pat may have been coaching his team, but in any case Adam was the star and his absence was glaring. I rode shotgun as Pat drove straight to the local hangout spot, a 7-Eleven. He would have made a good cop or detective. He parked, got out, walked to a low cinder-block wall bordering the lot, and peered over. He then reached down and stood up holding Adam by one arm like an obstetrician with a newborn. Adam was shirtless and the cinder blocks scraped his side, which was upsetting, though purely collateral. I considered it justified. We drove back to the field in shaken silence and Adam hit a homerun as if in defiance.

But that was the end of his boyhood dalliance with pot. For the moment.

The Parable of
Mr. Sunset

Once a year in the first half of the 1970s there was surfing on TV with the broadcast of the Duke Kahanamoku Invitational. For an hour or so and at a certain cost to its coolness, surfing was on par with professional tennis and golf, with the Miami Dolphins and the Olympic Games.

The perennial favorite was Jeff Hakman, whose dominance at the break earned him the honorific "Mr. Sunset." Hakman had the heavy-jawed looks of a handsome football player—open-faced and glowingly fit, somehow clean-cut despite his longish hair: a nice young man, a quarterback. He seemed, if you scanned the ranks of his generation, the least likely top surfer to become a raging heroin addict, though that's in fact what happened.

Hakman was born in 1948 in Redondo Beach to free-spirited, outdoorsy young parents whose idea of a vacation was riding motorcycles up the coast or camping in remote Mexico provisioned only with fishing gear and

bags of rice. When he was twelve, the family moved to
Oahu. Encouraged by his hard-charging father, Hakman
rode huge Sunset Beach and Waimea Bay as a pipsqueak
thirteen-year-old, astonishing the small group of hellmen
who had pioneered the breaks and were still often the only
ones who rode them. He won his first major contest—the
inaugural Duke of 1965—as a high school senior, surfing
so brilliantly that the judges had no choice but to give him
the victory over a field of legendary favorites in their prime.
Thus an addict-to-be like Hakman begins with an attrac-
tion to things that underscore the fact of choice, of being
set apart by daring to do what most others would not. But
freedom has a way of becoming its opposite, when the god
of the crossroads plays the trick of equivalence, making one
dare like another.

Hakman had an appetite for intoxicants but hardly an
outsized one, with beer and pot giving way to LSD in the
late 1960s as he entered his twenties. Like many surfers of
the era, he had fabulous, mystical sessions while tripping—
seeing through the clear backs of waves at Honolua Bay
the silhouettes of surf buddies racing along like phantoms
in another dimension. Yet "acid casualties" were a real and
terrifying phenomenon, as Hakman witnessed firsthand:
his friend and housemate Jackie Eberle, who had placed
second in the 1967 Duke, wandered off one acid-soaked
weekend on Maui in 1969, finally turning up Monday evening. When Hakman and Jock Sutherland woke him the
next morning, Eberle stared at them blankly. At the end of
the day Hakman and Sutherland found Eberle sitting in the
same position on the bed. Within a year he was institutionalized. Deeply shaken, Hakman swore off psychedelics.

He went on to win every major contest in the first half of the 1970s, but the purses were so small, the competitions so infrequent, and the clothing sponsorships so minor that he gave surf lessons in order to make ends meet. He also tried his hand at smuggling—hash from Afghanistan, pot from Mexico, and then, disastrously, Thai stick from Thailand, packed in stereo equipment and shipped via a US army base. But the DEA was watching, and Hakman, wretchedly nervous for weeks, avoided serious prison time only when the case was eventually dismissed on a technicality.

On a trip to Bali in 1975, he was startled to find surfers in his circle "chasing the dragon"—smoking heroin off foil. This was one drug Hakman had steered carefully clear of, frightened by its deadly reputation. Two top young surfers in Hawaii, Tommy Winkler and Rusty Starr, had died of overdoses, and later the Australian Kevin Brennan.

Hakman was twenty-seven in 1975, an era in which no one competed past the age of thirty. He was beginning to contemplate life after professional surfing, whatever that might mean. The story of his winning the Duke as a teenage prodigy had appeared in *Time* magazine. Where others had been busted for drug smuggling and gone to prison, he'd narrowly escaped; where others had been sent into the meat grinder of Vietnam, he'd tricked the draft-board examiners into believing he was unfit. Hakman was the golden boy swathed in an aura of luck, talent, and courage. But what now? Nothing had yet presented itself.

The heroin in Bali, meanwhile, was plentiful, cheap, and potent. The psychic space he crossed when he picked up the straw to take his first hit was categorically different from the space he crossed when he swung his board around and paddled for his first big wave but under the spell of the crossroads god must have appeared essentially the same: a gamble, a rush. "I remember this hammer hitting my spinal column," Hakman said later, "and a warm rush coming through my whole system. No drug had ever come close to making this kind of impression on me."

Was heroin simply the pharmacological key that fit Hakman's biochemical lock? Would he have become addicted whenever, wherever he tried it—earlier in his life, later? I think a constellation of factors had to emerge: uncertainty, economic precariousness, the nihilism and hedonism flowing from the Vietnam War. These were the stars above Uluwatu.

After Bali, Hakman traveled to Australia to compete in the iconic Bells contest. Big hippie sweaters and bell-bottom jeans worn by the back-to-the-land long-haired locals, gorgeous women, and hard-partying matey blokes, long right-hand point waves. He smuggled in two ounces of coke in the hollowed-out fin of his surfboard, traded some of it for heroin, and won the Bells competition blasted on both. The after-party went on and on but as drug-addled as Hakman was, he shrewdly perceived a business opportunity in the trunks made by Quiksilver and over dinner at a restaurant persuaded its founder to give him the licensing rights to make them in the United States, which entailed eating a paper doily as proof of his seriousness.

Back in California, the fledgling company flourished by dint of Hakman's initial dedication, but success in business failed to address a deeper craving and keep at bay the despair that had begun to seep in around the edges of things. He was making money now, but he was only making money. Hakman had ridden thirty-foot Waimea alone at first light. All the money in the world could not buy that—or bring it back to life. But money could buy a key of China White and that may not have been thirty-foot Waimea, but it was all right.

There followed a fifteen-year period in which Hakman's golden aura was burned away as by cigarettes during a nod: binges followed by grueling days of long withdrawals—cold sweats, nausea, aching, hopelessness—suffered through while holed up in hotels or on intercontinental flights or in apartments with the blinds drawn; lies to friends and lovers and business colleagues; hasty selling of real estate and valuable shares in the business he had built and finally embezzling from it in order to keep himself in heroin; hepatitis from sharing needles; second and third chances squandered; scheming, duplicity, poverty, mistrust, humiliation, loss of reputation, suicidal thoughts, old friends eyeing him warily.

What did surfing have to do with all of this? Was there, in Hakman's view, a connection? "I wouldn't go so far as to say letting go of the belt is like dropping into 30-foot Waimea," he says in an interview in 2004. "That instant of dropping down a big gnarly face—it's very close, equally potent, but not the same. On the other hand, the same thing that got me addicted definitely made me a good surfer. You know, once you get a direction, you go and commit." He pauses again. "I thought I could handle it," he says. "But every addict thinks that—that they're different."

Unlike Andy Irons, Hakman finally got fully and decisively clean, in a posh rehab facility in London, which was paid for by a friend and business colleague at Quiksilver who could not abide simply firing the great Jeff Hakman for his latest relapse, though the friend had vowed to do just that. And perhaps it was this demonstration of stubborn, unconditional love that brought Hakman back from the underworld. He had been admired and envied, but had he been loved for himself, apart from his cachet as a champion? Had he been waiting for the world to show that to him before fully committing to life after youthful glory?

The addiction may also have run its course. In any case, there was nothing of Hakman's golden aura left to burn.

"You know what finally really did it for me?" he says in an interview in 2020. "I just really want to surf good waves. It's such a thrill for me, and it's something that makes me feel *so good*. And to do that, I can't do any of this other stuff."

He lives on Kauai in a kind of surf-legend afterlife— Hanalei Bay as the Elysian Fields.

The Dark Road

On graduating from high school, the posse of local surfers I look up to scatter—to college, to California, to Kauai, to the rural stretch of coast near Sebastian Inlet that we call "down South." It's all very run-of-the-mill, this diaspora, but for me it's like the sudden loss of my tribe, as if they'd been killed in a raid. With no one above me in the water, no elders to witness and validate my performance, to model my behavior on, I feel disoriented and ghostly.

I begin riding my bike to the boardwalk in Indialantic, the neighboring town to the north, with Adam trailing close behind. Here there are crowds of surfers, along with tourists who watch us with wonderment and we pretend not to see. It's exciting to vie for waves with strangers, to assert oneself from scratch again and again, but it's an impersonal, urban sort of experience. What I long for (until I forget I do) is the intimacy I knew among the departed locals of my own beach, which will not come again.

The boardwalk is the domain of a swaggering, smooth-talking hipster whose shop is stocked with boards bearing his name, Dick Catri. Introduced to surfing at nineteen, in

1959, by diamond smuggler Jack Murphy, aka "Murph the Surf"—an underworld type Catri was drawn to—he spent the next five years on Oahu working as a lifeguard, apprenticing himself to legendary shaper Dick Brewer, and becoming the first East Coaster to ride Pipeline and Waimea Bay. He also competed in the 1967 Duke Kahanamoku Invitational at Sunset Beach. Having made his bones, Catri returned to the Space Coast and opened the first surf shops in the area, assembling teams of young surfers who rode his boards and often went on to become surf-world-famous themselves.

I know only the broad outlines of this story but feel the full force of Catri's charisma and authority when loitering around the shop, gazing at the framed photos of him riding North Shore waves, stroking the rails of the gleaming new boards. I would "surf for" Catri, too, I decide. I join the Eastern Surfing Association and enter contests in the boys division, which I win with relative ease, since there are only ever two or three others surfing against me, one of them usually Adam. The nigh self-published nature of these victories is a little absurd and shameful, but the trophies I place carefully on a shelf in my room have the talismanic power of official history, gradually eclipsing the squalid truth in a narcotic glow.

A year passes, two years. Surfing at the boardwalk one morning, I glance back toward shore and spot Catri's distinctive silhouette. He's sitting on a bicycle watching—watching me, I'm pretty certain. I begin to hunt down wave after wave in a kind of controlled frenzy. It's going to happen, he's going to take up my cause, tap me. Verily, I'm hired to work as the ding repairman in Catri's factory. I'm fourteen now, an apprentice. I will learn to make boards myself. I will emigrate to Hawaii.

A few weeks later Catri is busted for selling two hundred pounds of pot to an undercover cop. The factory is shuttered. Catri goes to jail.

I RISE IN the dark before school, creep out of the house, and ride my bike to the beach with my board under one arm. The ocean is the red and orange of the sky, the waves neither good nor bad though emphatically sharky at this hour. I go out in most any conditions now, often alone, like someone walking onto a court in an empty gymnasium. Surfing has quietly become a vocation, a pre-profession. I feel obscure twinges of regret about this conversion, but I don't know why. What's the alternative?

AROUND AND AROUND New Smyrna Beach, Pat speed shifts, sighing through his nose. There's a contest being held at an inlet here, but as in a bad dream we can't find it. Miserably I knead a puck of Sex Wax like a rosary and peer ahead in the hope of seeing cars and vans with surf racks, but there's only empty road and occasional glimpses of water through the trees. I wouldn't normally ask or expect Pat to drive a hundred miles early on a Saturday morning, but I need to surf in this contest in order to qualify for the East Coast Championships.

Pat knows something I don't: soon there will be no

possibility of surfing. Thus his resentment of having to en-
dure my futile résumé feathering, of finding himself lost.
At last we come to the inlet, but there's no sign of a contest,
only fishermen casting from a jetty into ocean as flat as a
bay. There can't be a surf contest without surf. The puck
of Sex Wax is as wide and thin as a pancake from all my
kneading. On the drive back to Melbourne Beach, I tear its
translucent meat to bits.

DAYBREAK ON THE coastal highway north, September 1975.
With me in the back of the van are men I worked alongside
during my brief stint as ding repairman in Catri's factory,
specialists in one or another aspect of surfboard manufac-
ture: shaper, glasser, glosser, sander. We sit like migrant
workers knee to knee, lie on sleeping bags spread over the
floor. Released from prison after serving thirteen months,
Catri himself is ferrying us to the East Coast Championships in Cape Hatteras.

Prison has changed him. His swagger is intact but lackluster. The flesh hangs heavier from the bones of his face.
He is more thoughtful, no longer reflexively cocksure. But
this is a road trip. To the beat of a song on the tape deck,
Catri bangs the heel of a hand on the steering wheel. He's
leaving behind the scenes of his disgrace and recent efforts
to redeem himself in the eyes of the community, such as
sponsoring a surf contest at my junior high school. All that
good-citizen bullshit can be flicked away like a cigarette
butt and forgotten for a few days.

Strapped to the roof racks among the other boards is a
yellow "plate" Catri allowed me to carry out of the shop

free of charge. I had bought two previous boards at cost but to be given one outright was a momentous step. But I had no sooner taken it than the ladder was kicked away.

Radiation, the company that hired Pat in DC and brought the family to Florida; whose offices he commuted to every weekday morning with unswerving regularity, driving across the Indian River on the causeway to Melbourne, then back across in the late afternoon or early evening; the company that sponsored our Little and Junior League baseball teams, which Pat coached, and whose eerie name appeared in red lettering on the uniforms; the taken-for-granted source of our income and material comforts: one day Pat no longer had a job there.

There were external factors—the oil crisis and the economic recession; the implementation of a merger with Harris Corporation. But Pat believed it came down to his having fallen out of favor with his boss. To be rid of him, the boss put Pat in charge of a new division that was likely to fail, and when it did, Pat was blamed and let go.

He told my mother later that he cleaned out his office and drove back across the causeway. It was late morning when he got home. The boys were at school, she was out somewhere with the baby. He fetched his rifle from the master-bedroom closet. He sat on the edge of the bed, unzipped the case, and slipped the rifle out. Sunlight filled the bedroom. He set the butt on the carpet between his feet and rested the underside of his chin on the barrel. A car passed slowly on the street outside. He thought then of his baby boy, of the consequences that would flow from this wound like blood. He sat for some time then slid the rifle into its case, zipped the case closed, and put it back in the closet. For the moment.

There followed a heady period in which he planned to keep us in Melbourne Beach by opening a family restaurant. I would wait tables, Adam would bus, our mother would be hostess. We spoke of it as an established reality, but in the end no bank would loan him the money—neither for a restaurant nor a skate park, the other, less plausible, scheme—and Pat accepted an offer from Boeing in Wichita, Kansas, the city where he grew up.

He's there now, having gone ahead to buy and ready a house for the family's arrival. I strain to hold the two realities on a single plane in my mind: Catri in the van; Pat in Wichita; Florida, Kansas; ocean, plains.

Catri has stopped somewhere in Cocoa Beach and disappeared into a high-rise apartment building to pick up a friend, who takes the shotgun seat when the two of them finally climb into the van. Whatever else he may be, the friend is not a surfer. As Catri pulls onto A1A, the friend bends over something, eventually turning to hold out a straw and a hand mirror where half a dozen lines are laid out: the sight is thrilling and alarming, like a brandished handgun.

But it's etiquette merely, the offer, and when no one accepts, the friend rescinds the mirror. Catri and his friend seem foolish to us, like incorrigible children. I have no inkling of my latent bond with them, our dormant brotherhood.

Hard rain crackles on the windshield. Jacked on coke, Catri and his drug buddy trade off driving the however many hours it takes to get from the Space Coast to the Outer Banks—all day. We check into a motel at Lighthouse Park Beach and surf at dusk on a building hurricane swell.

With the blast of an airhorn, the contest begins the next morning in big, heaving surf. Cape Hatteras sits on the edge of the continental shelf and waves arrive mainly undiminished, breaking so hard in such shallow water that sand sprays out their backs. I watch a surfer named Rick Rasmussen from New York—New York? They surf there?—kick-stall inches from the rusty steel groyne and pull into a meat-grinding barrel. Only the tip of the nose of his board is visible for an improbable stretch, then the wave shuts down like a piano lid.

Raz, everyone calls him. He had won the US Championship here in Cape Hatteras the year before, when he was nineteen, the first East Coaster to take a national title. Watching him, you instantly see the superiority of all-out risk, of going as fast as possible and keeping the board constantly on rail, pulling into a pit without a flicker of hesitation. It hardly matters that this time Raz is eliminated early and the strategically cautious surfers advance.

I don't remember when I learned that he was shot dead at age twenty-seven, in 1982, blond, blue-eyed Raz, doing a drug deal in Harlem. It was sometime after I had quit surfing and before I started up again in New York City. Of surfer deaths, it remains the bleakest and unlikeliest— aware though I am of how the sparks of the headline shower from the collision of stereotypes embedded in "Harlem" and "surfer." I pictured a strung-out and unstreetwise Raz somehow alarming an edgy dealer but as ever the truth was stranger and more baroque.

His father was a Marine Corps pilot who retired to fly for Grumman Aerospace Corporation, making an impression in Westhampton when he ate glass in a local bar.

Having played semipro basketball, Bill Rasmussen hoped his son would follow, but when the family moved to Long Island from Maine, Raz learned to surf on a pop-out longboard his older sister had been given after seeing *Gidget*. He was ten. Everything else fell away. Wearing a too-thin red-and-gold wetsuit (the Marine Corps colors), Raz surfed the Westhampton jetty breaks alone in deep winter, running home with chattering teeth and ice-clotted eyebrows to take a hot shower then running back to the beach. There were other surfers in Westhampton, but no one on the order of Dick Catri, living proof that someone from this backwater could run with the big dogs. Raz was sui generis.

He dropped out of school in the tenth grade and spent time surfing in Puerto Rico, the North Shore of the East Coast, rising rapidly through the amateur ranks, though the US title in 1974 was his competitive apogee: in the few pro contests he entered later, he fared poorly. In Hawaii, he found it impossible to get the waves he wanted at Pipeline, with its strict pecking order and threat of violence for dropping in. On a big borrowed board Raz paddled outside the lineup and sat pouting for an hour, like the new kid morosely kicking dirt in the far reaches of a playing field. Suddenly a huge second-reef wave loomed and feathered. Swinging the big board around, he caught it easily, turned off the bottom, and entered the enormous barrel from behind the peak. Photos of the wave appeared in surf magazines and later in the era-defining film *Free Ride*. For this and other barrels, Raz was given the nod by the reigning Pipe hellman, Gerry Lopez, and entered the VIP lounge.

That summer he traveled to Bali, surfing Uluwatu and the long, fast, drainpipe-hollow lefts at a newly established, exclusive surf camp in Grajagan, Java, called G-Land, which was built and run by American Mike Boyum, a legendary surfer–drug runner who quaffed magic-mushroom smoothies and fasted for better health and spirituality. The G-Land camp, including the various bribes and fees for its operation, had been paid for with money Boyum made smuggling Afghani hash oil into the United States. The main structures were stilt tree houses built high above the jungle floor, where tigers and other big cats prowled at night. Boyum later spent four years in a New Caledonia prison on drug charges and died on the forty-third day of a fast at the site of another perfect wave he discovered in the Philippines and named Cloud Nine.

Raz shipped half a ton of Balinese clothing and merchandise to Westhampton and opened an import-export business; he shaped boards under the, in retrospect, laughably wholesome Clean & Natural label he registered. Mostly he traveled the world with his personal photographer girlfriend in high rock-star style, surfing one famous break after another. He had lost interest in a career as a competitive pro, which at the time entailed making and selling boards and patching together sponsorships in order to travel on a tight budget to some far-flung contest where the waves might well be bad and he might well be eliminated early.

If Raz ever seriously intended to run an import-export business or sell enough Clean & Natural boards to pay the rent, he soon thought better of it. He had set forth on the dark road. Why? He wanted to keep the feeling going, to extend the high of surfing, bring it ashore. For people of a certain temperament, smuggling was irresistible, so much easier than holding down a straight job or combination of jobs, than working one's way up the pecking order—smuggling was like the second-reef wave that loomed up out of nowhere: a gift from God to the bold.

But at some point Raz committed the cardinal sin of getting high on his own supply, or it was the other way around and he became addicted and then smuggling seemed the best and inevitable way to keep himself in heroin. Bali in the seventies. Surfers at loose ends. I don't want to go home yet. I want to stay in polytheistic wonderland. Once heroin takes hold, the high personal standards of fitness and health; of going for runs in the morning and eating well; of right living; of being sensitive to others, to what they feel, to what might be best for them and you; fall by the wayside. The absence of that light is the darkness of the dark road.

Measured strictly according to whether one got caught or not, or got caught for something relatively minor only after a good long run, it was possible to succeed on the dark road. Surfer Steve Bigler from Santa Barbara, who came in fourth in the US Championships of 1966, set forth on it around this time, the mid-seventies, and spent the next twenty years smuggling and surfing his way around the world until he was finally busted in 1996, at which point he did a bit over two years in prison. (Was it worth it?) Good smugglers were superstitious and wary, methodical and painstakingly nondescript in manner and dress. For many, "good" also meant running forms of cannabis, Thai stick, or Afghani hash, and eschewing heroin, which was sorely tempting due to how valuable it is in relatively small quantities compared to garbage bags of pot—but evil.

In mid-seventies Bali, when people went out at night to the Kuta bars, all two of them, they wore T-shirts, trunks, and flip-flops. Raz sported python boots, designer jeans, a stylish collared shirt, and a scarf. He was a star, US champ, second-reef charger; he could not comport himself otherwise. But the star and his personal photographer girlfriend were arrested for possession of a kilo of cocaine and Raz spent three months in the notorious Kerobokan Prison awaiting his trial. His father wired $54,000 to Bali and when the case finally came before a judge, Raz was acquitted and released.

Two years later, having been tapped to be the guide for an episode of *The American Sportsman* that focused on surfing in G-Land, Raz was back in Bali. Did memories of the bust and Kerobokan Prison incline him to keep a low profile? Leading a TV crew and luggage containing twenty surfboards, Raz approached the Ngurah Rai airport customs desk wearing sunglasses and a striped shirt and carrying a boom box that was playing Pink Floyd's "Money."

The following year he was busted along with four others in Remsenburg, one town over from Westhampton, for selling four ounces of nearly pure China White, street value half a million, to an undercover agent. The sting was over a year in the making. Raz thought he was going to get sixty thousand dollars and Rolling Stones studio tapes to use on the soundtrack of a surf movie he planned to produce. He was released from jail when his ever-loyal father, drawing on his retirement fund, put up the million-dollar bail. In order to reduce the severity of his sentence, Raz began working as an informant, whereupon the road grew very dark indeed.

Ten months later, a week before he was scheduled to be sentenced, Raz drove to Manhattan with his girlfriend,

Jacquie, in a Mercedes sedan. It was her twenty-first birth-day. He had his sentencing to celebrate, too: he had been told that he would be given probation rather than prison time for his informant work. Raz would be getting his life back. He could start over. He was eager to try his hand at building windsurfing boards.

But Raz also had business to attend to: selling a pack-age of cocaine on behalf of a Westhampton dealer he was obliged to in some way. The call from the dealer had come that day. Raz had to move the coke by morning and he couldn't risk trying to sell it on Long Island, not with his law-enforcement handlers so close by. He broke this news to Jacquie at a sushi restaurant on the East Side of Man-hattan. He was sorry, he said, and apologized several more times during dinner.

New York City in 1982 remained that of the gritty, law-less 1970s: graffiti-covered subway cars, peep shows, and porn movie houses lining 42nd Street, hustlers of various kinds prowling the avenues, muggings at knife- or gun-point almost yawningly commonplace.

After dinner, Raz and Jacquie went to Xenon, a lesser Studio 54, on West 43rd Street. Having had no luck find-ing a buyer there, they got into the Mercedes sedan. It was nearly midnight. Raz had traveled the world. He had done drug deals abroad. But when it came to the flash and decep-tion of Manhattan, its quicksilver, shifting realities, he was still just a guy from Long Island.

Pulling into traffic, Raz noticed two young men in a black Toyota Celica. One of them was checking out Jacquie, Raz thought. He leaned into view and called to them.

"You got a problem?" the guy said.

"No," Raz replied, "no problem. Know anyone who'd be interested in getting some cocaine? I'll make it worth your while."

The other man in the Toyota was Vincent McCall. Originally from North Carolina, he had spent his early adolescence in Harlem, the protégé of a sixteen-year-old dealer who controlled the block. When McCall moved back to North Carolina in high school, he found himself among classmates who planned to go into professions like engineering or law. McCall became a serious student himself, joined ROTC, and won a scholarship to West Point. He liked to visit his old neighborhood in Harlem in his dress grays. He was a boxing champion at West Point but was forced to take a leave of absence in his junior year for accumulating too many disciplinary demerits. On the night he met Raz, McCall was living with an uncle on Columbus Avenue and could certainly have used the fixer money dangled by the blond dude. So could the friend in the car, Robert Mendez, an out-of-work carpenter who, of the five or six guys McCall had befriended during his time in Harlem, was the only one still alive.

McCall jotted his uncle's phone number on a slip of paper and passed it to Raz: Call later and they might have a buyer for him.

Back at the uncle's apartment, they talked about *The Sword and the Sorcerer* and whether the blond dude would call. McCall thought not—to him Raz seemed high on something and just acting the big shot for the sake of his girlfriend. Then the phone rang. It was Raz. Mendez told him to meet them at Columbus and 77th. Then he called a cabbie named Frank Angel, who was interested. Though how did they know this guy wasn't a cop? Cops buy, Mendez told him, they never sell.

August night in Manhattan. Anyone with a way to escape the sodden heat and ominously quiet streets was gone—to the Hamptons or the Jersey shore, Cape Cod or Maine, upstate. The only ones still here were the poor and dependent, junkies unable to leave their dealers, broke artists.

Sometime around 2:45 a.m. everyone convened at Columbus and 77th, McCall and Mendez in the black Toyota, Angel in his cab, Raz and Jacquie in the Mercedes sedan arriving just after. Raz got out and spoke to Angel and Mendez. Mendez then told McCall and Jacquie that Raz wanted to drive uptown. McCall was annoyed: this was getting too complicated. But uptown they went, Raz in the back seat of Angel's cab, Jacquie driving the Mercedes, McCall and Mendez in the Toyota. Angel began running red lights, panicking Jacquie, who raced to keep up. Meanwhile, McCall worried it might be some kind of setup.

At Riverside Drive and 152nd, Angel finally pulled over. Raz told Jacquie to keep the car running and went with Angel to the doorway of an apartment building then into the hallway. Angel must have sampled the coke. He later told McCall that he offered to buy three and a half grams and more later if he liked it. Raz was outraged, saying, "I only deal in large packages." How much did he mean by that—an ounce? Half an ounce? An ounce is twenty-eight grams; half an ounce, fourteen grams. Did Raz really think some stranger he met ten minutes ago was going to hand over however much a bundle that big would cost? He would have been lucky to sell three and a half grams. They came out of the building arguing.

Raz moved toward the Mercedes. He raised one arm. "Don't take my watch," he said. "Don't shoot my girl!" At the sound of gunfire Jacquie dropped to the floor of the Mercedes and looked up to see a pistol pointed at her. "Get the girl," someone said, but someone else said, "No, let's get out of here."

She found Raz lying on the sidewalk with a hole the size of a silver dollar below his left eye.

He was in a coma for sixteen days. Sitting vigil, his mother played Stevie Wonder tapes in the hope of bringing him back. On the day he died his right eye opened briefly: Westhampton, Puerto Rico, Cape Hatteras, Pipeline, Bali, Harlem.

There's too much freedom, my brother. But it's all a dream.

Look, it's already gone.

A Surfer in Kansas

To identify as a surfer so far from an ocean and with no hope of traveling to one with any regularity was too heartbreaking. I sold my boards before we left Melbourne Beach, gave away the stacks of *Surfer* and *Surfing*. Not long after arriving in Wichita, I sat in a barber's chair and had my long sun-bleached hair cut short. I lapsed into the feeling that stole over me when my parents split up: despair cut with anger and grief.

As time passed, I also felt a curious relief. Surfing was the worship of a whimsical, absentee god who nonetheless demanded total devotion when it materialized. The obligation to drop whatever else I might be doing when the waves came up exerted a continuous, subtly wearisome pressure. I was free of that now.

In Kansas, football was god—stolid, seasonal, unquestioned in its dominance. We arrived too late for me to play that fall, but I was big enough to attract the interest of the coaches. I began going to the weight room every day. I knew no one, I had nothing else to do. Endorphins swam buzzingly through my bloodstream after a few sets. I felt powerful, indomitable. The uprooting from Melbourne Beach had brought home to me that I had no say in where I lived and therefore what it was possible to be or become. In the weight room I resurrected the illusion of being in control.

Otherwise I read, book-club bestsellers, whatever came to hand—Michener, Haley's *Roots*, Irving Stone, Updike, Barbara Guest, *Watership Down*, Hesse's *Demian*. I had always been a reader but as in a waiting room, prepared to set the book aside when it was announced that the ocean would see me. Now I read with urgency, as a means of survival. I read on the school bus, I read under the noses of high school instructors giving lessons, I read in the cafeteria, I read at home in my room alone, with a record playing on the turntable and the music as the soundtrack of the narrative. It was not escapism, or not exactly. There was an element of cocreation, of working with the words in order to coax out the meaning, a lucid dreaming. I was in and aware of the world, but the cold factuality of it—the flat grid of Wichita, the stolid natives, the dead yellow grass of midwestern winter—was slightly distanced, softened, made subject to revision. Reading as a drug, the reader's head tipped forward like a junkie's. Reading while walking, while writing a letter to a friend in Melbourne Beach. Reading while reading.

I'd been so indifferent to academics in junior high that my mother was advised to put me on a vocational track for high school. Whispered to by continuous reading, a dormant aspect stirred—the writer or poet. There were languages to learn on this path, philosophy, monuments of culture. Though also ghoulish figures—staggering drunk

Dylan Thomas; Virginia Woolf walking into the Ouse with stones in the pockets of her overcoat; John Berryman with his long fingernails and piss-stained trousers leaping from a bridge; Hart Crane, from a ship into the Caribbean after neatly folding his coat; Ernest Hemingway and his shotgun; Sylvia Plath with her head in the oven; Anne Sexton inhaling car exhaust; Robert Lowell and James Schuyler in straitjackets. Burroughs on smack, Kerouac on Dexedrine and booze. Western art and literature for the past two hundred years on one thing or another—caffeine, cocaine, laudanum, alcohol, tobacco, amphetamine, peyote, mushrooms, acid.

I metabolized this moral so completely that many years later, when I finally and decisively quit, it was like psychic surgery: I had to plunge into and seize myself, drag me out of the underground stream of this story about the drunken, visionary poet into which I had waded blind, becoming a votary of it, someone in whose veins flowed intoxicants. I rested on the bank beside myself, watched as I opened my eyes and sat up.

In the spring I began working out with the football team. I'd put on thirty pounds and looked like I'd been lifting weights in prison. I made first-string defense but found I'd lost not only whatever quickness I had but any passion for actually playing. Weight training had become an end in itself, the way cocaine later eclipsed the writing it was originally enlisted to aid.

For my sixteenth birthday my mother gave me Transcendental Meditation lessons. My instructors were a pair of mild-mannered Wichita State University graduate students greeting me at the door of a Victorian house in stockinged feet. The meditative state was familiar—like the trance I entered after reading for an hour or two, or when I floated on a surfboard, breath shallow and slow, and gazed at the horizon. But you don't need a book or the ocean. You don't even need the vehicle of the mantra. Meditation is about letting the world fall away, fall silent. Though not always twice a day as prescribed, and with hiatuses sometimes lasting months, I've meditated ever since. It's helped me to regulate and gather myself, especially for a concentrated effort or shift, like getting sober.

With the approach of my seventeenth birthday, I was allowed to accept the standing invitation from my best friend and his mother to live with them in Melbourne Beach. My dependency on that oceanic world, my identification with it, had been broken by distance and time. Now I was permitted to go back as if that severance had been the condition of any return.

I said goodbye to my mother the night before I left. I was going away when she would need me most, but neither of us knew that then. Pat drove me to the airport early in the morning. It was late December and still dark, the roads empty. We said little, but there was a glowing sense of peace and acceptance between us—love, really. He told my mother about it, which surprised me a little, given how guarded he usually was. "Most people," he said, "are like this"—he drew two separate circles on a piece of paper. "In the car, Thad and I were like this—" And he drew two circles that overlapped almost completely.

He began drinking again in the new year. The relief of having landed a good job in the wake of losing one had faded, I imagine. What remained was Wichita, high school classmates popping up at the pharmacy or hardware store, hearing himself tell his story tailored to the person and the moment, though he suspected they always saw through to the simple truth: he had failed to make it in the wider world. That was worse, he decided, than never having set forth, which had the virtue of modesty and dignity. But ultimately I suspect it had nothing to do with where he was, or even with success or failure. He carried it from place to place, year to year. It was inside, like a parasite, and he could not rid himself of it.

During an argument late at night, having come home drunk, he began to strike my mother. The next day he wrote her a letter pleading for forgiveness and they made up, but he kept drinking. One night he stayed out so late that she gave up waiting for him and went to bed alone.

She woke with a start, she told me later. He was moving through the bedroom, out into the hallway.

Pat? she called. She felt suddenly certain that he was going to murder her and the children.

What's going on? she called. Pat?

The phone rang: it was the police. They had found him in his car on the side of a road. He had killed himself with a rifle.

I WAS IN the house of my best friend and his mother, in a bedroom on the second floor, reading. It was quiet. My best friend was at his girlfriend's. His once fearsome stepfather, a retired air force colonel, had moved out. Divorce was in the air. The colonel still drove a Cadillac with a horn that played "La Cucaracha," but the festive days of blowing it as he tooled around town were past. Stooped and shrunken, the colonel was drinking himself to death.

It was mid-April. The surf was rideable though not good enough to tempt me away from my book, even with the added appeal, on the lanai, of a swallowtail Catri had recently shaped for me. I'd bought it at cost but with the tacit suggestion that if I proved myself in competition, the previous arrangement—free boards—would be restored. I had renewed my membership in the Eastern Surfing Association and entered a contest slated for the following month at the Indialantic boardwalk.

Still, I did not rise in the dark and paddle out before school, surf in whatever waves. It was often windblown and cold that winter and early spring, with no one else in the water. No one was on the beach either, or perhaps just a man in a windbreaker and canvas hat combing the sand with a metal detector. Black flies rising from mounds of Sargasso seaweed; the poisonous blue of a Portuguese man-of-war's flotilla; clots of tar.

I could live without the ocean and surfing. That was the lesson of Kansas. There was life after that death by removal, and I no longer felt the same attachment to this oceanic world and its values. There was another world, that of the mind, the realm of no place. But today my immersion in the book wavered. I was aware that it was overcast and dull out. I was a little depressed, perched on the bedspread that had been pulled taut by a housekeeper, conscious of myself as isolate, curled in the biosphere of myself. It had made sense in Wichita, this form. Why was it still intact?

The phone rang then fell silent. I heard the tread of my best friend's mother approaching in the hall. She knocked on the open door. "It's your mom, honey."

A touch of coolness in her voice. There had been a dispute over the cost of my upkeep. My mother had threatened to recall me to Wichita.

I picked up the phone.

It was the last thing I expected to hear from her. I thought: Dead?

What could kill that man?

BACK IN WICHITA the summer following Pat's death, I tunneled more deeply into books, into reading as trance state. A void had opened along the edges of things. You could just make it out at the corner of your vision. My mother joined a New Age Christian group called Emissaries of the Divine Light.

Pot smoke seeped out of Adam's room. He was like a tiny nation after the toppling of a strong man. He had always been eccentric—obsessive, fastidious, willful. When he was a boy there was a sweet side to it: he moved his bed into the baby's room in order to be there if he cried and became Jason's constant companion. His perfectionism lent itself to the repetition compulsion of skateboarding. He appeared, at age eleven, in a Who's Hot column in *Skateboarder* magazine. In Wichita, hoping to capitalize on the spread inland of the sport, Pat and our mother opened a small store, selling the new wheels and trucks and boards, and Adam was suddenly the star of the family, with a promotional excuse to hop on his board in parking lots and courtyards, running through his freestyle routine—handstands, 360s, nose wheelies—as the Kansans gawped. The aloof, rock-star persona that grew out of these performances turned colder and more grandiose in the wake of Pat's death. He carried around our mother's copy of *The Seth Material* and affected occult knowledge. He expected to be acknowledged as some sort of boy guru and was gloweringly offended by skepticism, especially mine.

My mother sent him to live with our father in DC, where he smoked pot openly, befriended outcasts, and strained our father's second marriage to the breaking point. A boy sitting behind him in Deal Junior High School threatened in a whisper to take his skateboard until Adam stood up and hit him across the head with it: Here, it's all yours. He was suspended for fighting and eventually returned to Wichita.

It was in this period that he first said he wanted to die. He discovered acid.

ON THE EVE of flying back to Wichita for Pat's funeral and prepared to remain there if my mother asked me to, I was introduced to a girl I would date for the next two years. The circumstances infused our meeting with high drama, but the relationship itself was characterized by routine—of school, of her part-time job in an insurance agency, and of her father, a Vietnam vet who taught at a military academy and spent the evenings and weekends parked in a Barca-Lounger watching TV and drinking beer.

Still in the picture initially was an ex-boyfriend who also had a drinking problem. When they went to the movies, she told me, he brought a bottle along. She was trying, with the last of her influence, to get him to attend AA meetings. She set forth a tenet of the program as established fact: an alcoholic is always and forever an alcoholic, even if he or she is sober and hasn't had a drink in decades—an idea I argued against in an idle, academic spirit, seeing no connection to my own life.

Meanwhile, we drank six-packs of Miller High Life as we listened to Marvin Gaye's *Live at the London Palladium*, wine with restaurant dinners, many daiquiris at the disco where a white funk band played the same set note for note, night after night.

In my comeback contest at the Indialantic boardwalk, I fared poorly, unable to shake off an inhibitory self-consciousness, to regain my former sense of entitlement and affront at being challenged in competition.

Divorced from the colonel, my best friend's mother sold the family house in Melbourne Beach and we moved to a condominium on the beach in Indialantic. The view of the ocean from the fifth-floor balcony was grand but unflattering to the waves, which appeared smaller and flatter from on high. When the retirees who lived in the other apartments complained about the presence of my board in the elevator and my dripping trunks, I was relegated to climbing the stairs. I found myself surfing less.

"Don't imagine you're too familiar," sang Billy Joel on my girlfriend's car stereo, but I did imagine it as I rode with her to the community college where she was taking accounting classes to please her father, read in the library while she flirted with a handsome classmate in the stacks, learned the nautical knots to help her pass the final exam of a sailing class. I sat beside her on the living room floor and watched her watch her soap opera. I listened to Billy Joel.

The alternative was free fall—weightlessness, drift, vertigo: empty public racquetball courts where I practiced alone in the afternoons, the report of a well-hit ball like a gunshot; the vast sky at dusk above the Indian River— brooding purples and indigos, smoldering apricots and pinks being engulfed by unfathomable darkness.

A white-haired neighbor invited us over for cocktails. He had been the official White House photographer during the Kennedy years. Paging proudly through a coffee-table compilation of his work, he glanced at me as if doubtful of my ability to grasp the achievement. Outside, the light of another day was dying, the gory hues seeping into the tidy, comfortable living room. The former White House photographer was living out his sunset years, but the actual sunsets were Wagnerian and I was drowning in their blood.

Between Waves

Washington, DC, early morning, early 1980s. I'm making coffee in the lower level of the Dupont Circle duplex where I live with my girlfriend, a singer-songwriter from a large, warm, musical family in which I have the place of unofficial son-in-law. The patriarch, now an attorney, was a congressman for twenty years. Their house in Georgetown is a world of taste and tradition, where my father's being a professor of classics is accorded great respect while surfing goes unmentioned and untranslated as it fades into the past.

My romance with the singer-songwriter, who is a few years my senior, has been of the purest, most idealistic kind. But since she graduated from the university where we met and began to teach in a private school, a mood of uncertainty has entered into things. Here at the start of summer, she's gone to New Hampshire to visit her younger sister for a month, maybe longer.

Meanwhile, I've taken on more hours at my job in the circulation department of the university library. It's something I've thought I might do full-time once I get my own

BA next year. A humble, anonymous job that doesn't require all or even much of me, which leaves my mind free for poetry and reflection. I don't want to analyze or argue or describe anymore. I just want to be.

But being is hard. Solitary days pass in which I barely speak. Reshelving volumes in the silence of the stacks, I've felt myself detach, the balloon of self drifting slowly up and away from earth, an earth without purchase or handhold or necessary relation. I find myself gazing at the large gleaming eyes of an animal in a book of wildlife photographs. I yearn to have or be what those eyes seem to embody: exemption from thought and intention, from the persistent low-grade suffering endemic to human experience, human consciousness.

Drawn by a faint chittering noise, I glance up from my coffee and jump at the sight of someone crouching outside the ground-floor windows: Adam—blond mohawk, leather, mascara on his eyes. He grins and goes down the stairs to the basement door to be let in, like a stray cat that knows the way.

He moved to DC a year after I did. He lived in our father's house when I was still there, working as a male stripper, much to everyone's discomfort. During an acid trip he'd witnessed the death of his ego and was convinced he was enlightened. I mocked him mercilessly for it, but it was all he talked about, even at my girlfriend's house in Georgetown, where he laughed in the face of the matriarch when she tried to bring him around with basic Christian instruction.

After I moved in with the singer-songwriter, he met a

punk-rocker cocktail waitress from Baltimore who introduced him to crystal meth. They were married in the winter. Now she's kicked him out of their apartment. He spent
the night on a bench in Dupont Circle.

He stalks from room to room, breathing through his
nose like a bull, his aura electric and insane, the veins in
his muscles standing out.

He strips off his leather vest and washes his face and
upper body at the bathroom sink. I'm hovering to make
sure he doesn't hurt himself and at the same time on guard,
braced for whatever.

He looks at me in the mirror: We need to take a road
trip.

Sure, I say.

I flash on riding a Greyhound bus back to Melbourne
Beach, to the ocean.

You and me, Adam says. Road trip.

We wouldn't make it past Dupont Circle.

AFTER GRADUATING, I quit my job at the university library and
clerked at a bookstore, waited tables at a French restaurant.
Later, when I began to drink programmatically, in the tradition of poets and painters like Kerouac and Pollock, I
would occasionally lose track of time, not only the time
of day but the era. I once left a party and walked to the
apartment building where an ex-girlfriend had lived, expecting her to be there when she had moved to Europe years
before.

Now I got drunk on books about Paris in its artistic

heyday of the 1920s and 1930s. I was living hand to mouth. Why not do it there? With the blessing of the singer-songwriter, who was ready to see me go, I flew to Paris expecting to find it essentially as depicted in *A Moveable Feast* and *The Banquet Years*.

It was not. The storied bohemian districts were moribund, the iconic cafés overpriced and touristic. I met a few interesting fellow misfits, worked as an au pair in the suburbs. To write in a notebook of gridded paper surrounded by the white noise of a foreign tongue was stimulating. But my French eventually improved to the point that I understood: the talk in Paris was of New York and Berlin—the energy I sought had moved elsewhere. After less than a year away I returned to DC.

It was then that I sank without reserve into the despair that composed the soil of my addictions. I was reunited with the boy on the bench after the split of my parents. To be a poet—liminal, neglected, bereft—complemented him.

Lacking both the money and the nerve to move to New York City, I took a room in a group house in Adams Morgan and a job as a museum guard. The main appeal of the museum was that reading was permitted at the posts—until a few Giacometti figurines were filched, turning up on the front steps along with a note deploring the lax security. With reading banned, I sat listening to the needle of the air-control monitor scratching over its scroll of graph paper and clocked out at six feeling pickled.

Divorced from the punk rocker, Adam was living with an older woman who sold vintage clothes from a rack at the entrance to the Dupont Circle Metro stop, which was where he could be found—ranking on passersby with the catty girlfriend, running the occasional errand. He still wore the mohawk and ripped jeans, but his affect was that of a jester or trickster rather than a spiritual arsonist. For the moment.

He hopped down from his perch on a low wall and gave me a quick hug. I was no longer a "college boy," as he used to call me with a sneer—no longer floating above the earth in a bubble of privilege and promise. I had a decidedly menial job and no obvious prospects. We were equals again.

He conferred in a low voice with his girlfriend, who smirked, went into her purse, and handed him a bill. Loping away with a jaunty step, he tossed his head for me to follow. He liked to use me as a bodyguard when he went to buy pot or, more recently, "love boat," PCP.

A boy was riding a cheap beginner's skateboard. "Hey, could I try?" Adam asked.

The boy turned to a man, probably his father, who nodded.

Adam picked up the board, sniffed it, peered at the deck. "So you stand on the top part here, right?"

Before the boy could answer, Adam dropped the board and jumped on it in midair, the clack of the wheels ringing across the plaza. He slalomed among startled commuters, then ran through the old freestyle routine, ending with a whirl of 360s in front of boy and father, head tilted back, hands clasped at his chest. A small crowd had stopped to watch. The punk regalia made for good street theater.

He stomped on the board so that it shot upward, then stooped and caught it on his shoulders. "Oh, God, get it off!" he told the boy. "It's burning me! Somebody get it off!"

Grinning, the kid snatched away the skateboard.

It was a warm night. The cafés near Dupont Circle were filled with lawyers and bureaucrats and lobbyists. Adam attracted a lot of stares, but that was the point. I was the rock star's drab sidekick, his roadie. On 18th Street, where the bars were more bohemian, the reaction was more veiled but essentially the same.

Finally we turned onto a street as ominous as the click of a pistol being cocked. Neither of us spoke. The lights were dim and widely spaced, the houses shuttered and dark, the unpruned trees looming over root-erupted sidewalks. Nothing was moving, not a cat, not a rat, not a roach.

Adam pulled up and looked around, then led the way into a brick building whose side door was propped open with a blue high-top sneaker, the toe bent back. On the landing of the second floor, two teenagers sat with their backs against a metal door. We stopped a few steps below, like supplicants.

One of the kids raised his chin: What did we want?

"Dime of boat," Adam said in a small voice.

The kid held out his hand. Adam went to give him the bill, but I stopped him. "Where's the boat?" I asked.

"Inside. Money first."

"We don't know you," I said. "Why should we give you money?"

The kid shrugged. "You want the boat."

"You could just disappear in there."

As if to demonstrate, the kid got up and went through the door, which banged shut. Adam stared at it like a dog. The light flickered. Something rustled in a trash can.

The kid came back out. "They say money first," he said apologetically.

"Let's go," I told Adam.

Out on the street, Adam fretted. "Now what?"

"I don't know, but they could just take your money and wait until you gave up and left."

Adam spat and went back inside. I stayed put in protest, then followed and met him coming down the stairs.

He thrust a bit of tinfoil under my nose. "Jesus, it smells like embalming fluid!"

Adam gave a satisfied nod. "Love boat."

WORN DOWN BY wage labor and poverty, I did what I had vowed not to do and applied to PhD programs. My high-minded reasons for resisting this path, that poets and po-etry were being corrupted and rendered irrelevant by their dependence on the academy, seemed like the scruples of a bygone innocent era. I was the night clerk at a Georgetown hotel where the notable event of the week was the arrival of the dry-cleaning order of the Ethiopian prince in exile who lived in the penthouse suite. When I wasn't working, I was sleeping off hangovers. Little poetry, corrupt or pure, was getting written.

I turned the pages of glossy university catalogs—patrician phrasing, emerald lawns, sunlight tinted by stained glass falling on the pages of an open book. The concept of aca-demia I formed as a boy, in the company of my father and the professors on his side of the family, was essentially priestly—well-scrubbed bare feet in leather sandals, Jesu-itical hauteur combined with a kind of scholarly dryness. Their temperament was foreign, but the basic bookishness was familiar, familial. Perhaps their rarefied world was mine after all. Perhaps I was a priest, too—a hermetic poet-priest who would be given leave to vanish into a verbal, scribal world.

I wrote the application essay listening, over and over, to the nervously yearning opening bars of one of Beethoven's late quartets. In my imagination the university had morphed from bland corporate prison into monastic refuge. The possibility that its gates might open at my knock led me to cut back on my drinking almost unawares. It was the return of hopefulness, of rising as on incoming waves. As if I were an ocean and addiction what happened in the absence of swell, when I lay flat and eventually cast about for wave machines.

I was offered a full teaching fellowship by the English Department at Yale: monthly stipend, tuition for two years' coursework waived, then teaching undergraduate sections of lecture classes and freshman composition. I had toured the campus not long after applying. What I came away with as a kind of emblem of its august luxury were the deep blue leather chairs in the reading room of the Sterling Memorial Library, standing lamps casting a gentle light over books open in the hands of students. If I were so blessed as to be accepted, to be lifted out of the world of waiting tables and clerking, this is the room where I would spend my time, in one of those deep blue leather chairs.

"Welcome to the profession," the director of Graduate Studies said in her address to my class. If not at that moment, I realized early on that it was not the right place for me. There probably was none at the time—a right place or occupation. The deep blue leather chairs turned out to be oddly uncomfortable, the tasteful light of the lamps too dim for reading at length. But lacking any better ideas, and aside from the year I took a leave to live in New York City, I stayed put in New Haven for seven years. I passed the language exams in Latin, German, and French, the coursework, the oral exams. I wrote a dissertation. On its face, graduate school would seem to be the absolute antithesis of the beach world I came from, but they share something essential beneath the surface: being liminal—lowly, invisible, betwixt and between.

A new diner opens on Elm Street. It's the fall of 1990. I sit in a booth and write in a sketchbook. The youngsters working behind the counter are druggie enough to possibly have a connection. Eventually I ask and am told to wait while it's looked into. The clear autumn light pouring in through the pane glass acquires a hopefulness, a sense of improving luck, which gradually fades as the connection fails to call back or show up.

It's hard to get drugs here. The townies keep their distance and the Yalies work too hard. There's no need or no money, or if need and money, no connection. There's always the stoop of the house on Day Street, far from campus, but that takes a rare desperation. The sound of my footfall echoes in the silence as I walk quickly and always alone because no one else is so reckless.

In the sketchbook, a P becomes a Y, which becomes a Nike-like winged figure I repeat down the page. The winged figure becomes a squiggled hanged man then a very distinct elongated hanged man, the eyes canceled by a black bar, horizontal lines darkening the body like the wrappings of a shroud or mummy.

I draw five careful pincerlike nooses then a figure curled in a heap on the floor.

I'm unaccountably depressed.

TWO DAYS LATER my father calls to tell me that Adam has committed suicide—he hanged himself. He was twenty-seven.

I fly out to visit my mother in Montara, a town next to Half Moon Bay. We scatter Adam's ashes in Golden Gate Park, where he was homeless for a period.

The beach is just a block from the house in Montara. I walk there and sit on a rock and watch waves roll into the small cove without breaking.

NEXT DOOR TO us in Montclair is a house that was flipped—bought, torn down, rebuilt from scratch, and sold to a couple in their early thirties, high school sweethearts with a one-year-old daughter. The tightly wrapped husband we barely saw. He worked on Wall Street, rising like a soldier at five thirty to catch the early train to the city. About six months ago, at a bachelor party, he died. The widow's parents had told us that the cause was an undetected heart defect, but recently the widow confessed the truth: he was first among his buddies to do a line of what they thought was coke and died almost instantly from the effects of fentanyl.

I just came from the garage, having taken out the garbage while they are all away at the shore. It was very much the husband's domain, the garage, and I walked gingerly and with respect, as if at a gravesite. My eye lingered over the silver ratchet wrench and sockets in the tool box, the grille of a lacrosse helmet glinting on the concrete floor. I remembered the garage in Wichita after the death of Pat, another tightly wrapped husband, his workbench and tools hanging on clips stuck in a sheet of perforated masonry, the stillness of the objects, the aura around them of the man who had used them a certain number of times before dying.

I think of a trip I took to Mexico City, when I was in graduate school. On a whim I went to Puerto Escondido, unaware that in the years since I'd stopped paying attention to surfing the wave there had entered the canon, dubbed the Mexican Pipeline. The surf was so good that I rented a board, which a heavy close-out barrel soon snapped in half.

Walking on the beach later, I noticed a small triangular packet lying on the sand. Puerto was a party town. I picked it up—damp green tissue paper with about three grams of white powder inside. Cupping it in one hand, I went back to my hotel room.

I opened the damp paper and tapped some of the powder onto a plate. Then I stopped and stood there blinking. For all I knew, this could be rat poison. Was I going to snort it into my nose, into my brain?

I dumped the package and powder into a garbage can. I washed my hands at the sink and stood drying them slowly, returning to myself.

I was beginning to emerge at this stage. The addiction was like a dying fire or a fever. It had also no doubt helped that I had just been surfing.

There is a semiotic dimension to addiction, an interplay

between cognition and emotion that is activated by, in this case, the signifier *cocaine*. What I thought when I thought about it and felt as a consequence of that thought was losing coherence. It was like a printed symbol that had been exposed to the weather. Originally it meant control and self-containment, relief, power. As it faded over time, its capacity to convey that sense grew uncertain, required more effort to decipher, and what I felt was less coherent, less forceful.

What did cocaine mean to the serious young husband? Being a little allowably bad perhaps. Ritualized and sanctioned release from the tight grip of self-control, tinctured with a bit of danger, the street. The force of cocaine as a signifier was probably still crisp.

But I won't speculate about his death. His death is inscrutable.

PART II

Sandy Hook

The first hurricane of the season moves up the coast then swerves away. The swell is minor and the winds are howling, but I drive "down the shore," as they say in New Jersey, curious to see how a certain spot is reacting and just to stand close to the storm energy.

The sky streams with bands of low white clouds, the underbellies dark with rain. The guard huts at the entrance to the state park are vacant, the road leading to the parking lot, the parking lot itself. Scrub, rugosa rose, poison ivy, slab concrete restrooms, clumps of dried seaweed like snarled cassette tape tumbling past on the sand.

The ocean is gray-green, whitecaps flashing beneath a dark strip of sky at the horizon and the waves have a mad, tossing character, like open-sea chop. When they form up into something possibly surfable, the wind snatches at the whitewater and spews it into the air as through a blowhole.

I walk to the water's edge and sink past my ankles in swampy, high-tide sand. To the north is the lower Manhattan skyline, clearly visible even in this watery light. A photograph was taken more or less where I'm standing. Along the bottom is a black band on which is typed in white letters:

SEPTEMBER 11, 2001	IN MEMORY OF	9:15 A.M.

In the foreground, a scattering of seven or eight surfers in various relations to a wave—sitting up on their boards just past it, recovering from having been caught inside by it, paddling over it, turning away having failed to catch it. In the background, as in a vast diorama, the smoke rising from the towers looks like a monstrous gray tornado dropped down to feed upon them.

No one saw it coming is the story of that morning, but surfers had been eagerly expecting the arrival of this swell. Erin, the hurricane that spawned it, never threatened to make landfall and was mentioned by newscasters only in passing if at all. But it had come churning up the East Coast at such a leisurely, generative pace and the winds of a cold front set to groom it were so favorable that it was looking to be the best swell in a decade, albeit typically short-lived— just a day really, a feast with leftovers.

People were in the water at first light to catch the swell at its peak. I would have been, too, but I wanted to surf with my friend J., who had to drop his daughter at daycare at eight-thirty. I was on the faculty of a college in Brooklyn, and the one advantage of going so late was that I could leave a message on the voicemail of the English Department at a plausible hour of the morning: I'm afraid I need to cancel class today—not feeling well. Please put a note on the door of the room.

It was a call I made at least once every fall, but this year was different: I had just been named director of the writing program and today was the first day of classes. I certainly wanted to make a solid directorial debut, to justify the faith placed in me by my dean. Still, a class could be made up. A once-in-a-decade swell is a kind of evanescent natural wonder. When I pictured my freshmen reading the note on the door and turning away in disappointment, I felt a pang. But I was going surfing anyway. I could not not go.

Along with being named director, I had been given the keys to a faculty house on campus. At a front window I stared down the street in the direction J. would be arriving from. The weather was almost painfully beautiful. Students streamed past two and three abreast, faculty and administrators were pulling into the main parking lot. Living on campus meant you were often on view; there was no clear separation between work and nonwork. When J. pulled up, I would have to ford this river of students with my board under my arm. Nothing says *I'm ditching work* quite like strapping a surfboard to the racks of a car in the morning. Would someone notice, would word get around?

I was half listening to the local public radio station. An announcement came over the air of an incident of some kind, then the signal went out. My wife, Juliana, found the station on AM. A witness was reporting having seen a plane fly low across the city and then into one of the World Trade Center towers. I imagined a Cessna. We turned on the TV to an image of one of the towers with gray smoke pouring from a gash high up, like a fatal head wound.

I had worked in the World Trade Center, on the eighty-second floor, teaching English to Japanese businessmen.

I'd had to change elevators on the way up, as in a subway. I could remember the sunlight coming in through the narrow windows, the queasy sensation as the whole thing flexed and swayed in a high wind.

The phone rang. It was J. He had noticed smoke in the sky after dropping his daughter off. When he got back to his house to get his board, he went up to his attic and opened the roof hatch and saw a long streak of black smoke with bits of white in it—paper, he realized. It led all the way back to the tower. Then he sat down and wept for all the people who must be dying. He was weeping as he told me.

Then the second plane hit.

Classes were canceled. I walked over to the classroom and told my students in person, as if I had had every intention of being there on time to teach. Some of them went up onto the roofs of campus buildings—you could see Manhattan from there—and we heard their screams and shouts as first one then the other tower collapsed.

The next day I drove out to Long Beach in the car we had just bought when we moved to Brooklyn. People find it strange or worse that I went surfing the day after 9/11, but for me it was like going to church—like psychic medicine, like sacrament. I was thinking about surfers who had called in sick to their jobs at Cantor Fitzgerald and lived—the mystery of who lived and who died.

Having always ridden shotgun in J.'s car, I had never paid close attention to the route and wound up on one of the ring roads of JFK airport. When I realized my mistake, I made a U-turn in front of some kind of security booth. To the plainclothes cops staking it out, this sudden about-face looked highly suspicious and they sprang from hiding shouting and waving me down, four or five of them in sweatshirts and jeans and sneakers, peering in through the windows of the car. Where was I going, why had I turned around when I saw them?

"I got lost," I said helplessly, gesturing at my board where it lay in the back. "I'm just trying to go surfing."

A MOUND OF yellowish foam appears at my feet, trembles then breaks into pictographic bits, which stand quaking like an urgent message before being scattered. Sand swirls up in a small dust devil. I close my eyes, then open them. A wave bursts against a rock and a veil of mist falls over me.

Augustine rejected paganism on Platonic grounds: the natural world is subject to change and ultimately mortal, un-eternal, and therefore unworthy of worship. A swell is born and dies. The ocean itself will eventually die. But surfing has made me a pagan, a pantheist. The sun and sky and ocean have always been present in my experience, un-born, continuous.

This present summer is dying though, nearly over. It's legible in the angle and thinness of the light, a certain dryness in the air, how the wind sounds blowing across the sand.

Waves

The sun heats the earth, hot air collides with cold to make storms that blow their force into the ocean, which makes waves, tiny and separate at first, like millions of toy sailboats. The wider the area of the storm and the stronger the wind, the bigger the waves, which grow and merge and form small groups, like flotillas. Yet waves are not water. Waves are cylinders of storm energy that displace water, reaching into the depths as they roll along until they either dissipate or touch bottom, expiring a little on contact and moving ahead or, if the bottom is abruptly shallow, stumbling and tripping and heaving upward to break.

Big-storm energy rolling through the Atlantic spends itself in increments as it brushes against the shallow continental shelf, reaching the East Coast in waves that seldom exceed ten feet. Meanwhile, a submarine canyon off the northwest coast of Puerto Rico ushers in waves of twice that size.

Bathymetry is destiny, but all waves, however big, either fade away or run aground and break.

Yet waves are not water.

Brain Bathymetry

In a landmark 1988 study using positron emission tomography (PET) scanning, which permits researchers to view living human brains, Nora Volkow found decreased blood flow to the prefrontal cortex of cocaine addicts even ten days after withdrawal. The most recently evolved part of the brain, the prefrontal cortex governs executive functions such as planning, decision making, and inhibitory control. Volkow's study established that addicts faced with the choice of using or not using are unable to properly weigh the choice because addiction has in effect taken the prefrontal cortex offline. By flooding the brain in amounts unheard of in our evolutionary history, drugs like cocaine and heroin "hijack" the brain's reward circuitry, altering neurobiology. The consensus that emerged from this and other studies is that drug and alcohol addiction, rather than a matter of weakness of character or morality, is a chronic but treatable brain disease.

And while the disease model has been enormously beneficial to the cause of destigmatizing addiction, it has problems as science. There is no unique genetic or neurological pathology present in all addicts but absent in everyone else, for instance. No one can test positive for drug or alcohol addiction and whether a given individual will become an addict cannot be predicted. The definitional emphasis on changes occurring in the brains of addicts downplays the fact that it's the very nature of the brain to change in response to experience, including potentially undoing with new, healthy behavior what has been altered by previous patterns of drug misuse. Another challenge has emerged with the newly recognized class of "behavioral addictions" such as gambling, Internet, shopping, sex, and surfing, too, which can have an impact on the brain comparable to that of drug addiction, with the same destructive consequences—job loss, relationship collapse, financial ruin. Thus, drugs of abuse can no longer be accorded their special, supervillain status. There is clearly something more afoot.

According to Marc Lewis and Maia Szalavitz, addicts who got sober and went on to become addiction researchers, that something is learning—we learn addiction, learn that drugs give us pleasure and relief, help us to cope with feelings of dislocation and stress. For this reason a baby can't be "born addicted" to crack or opioids. The suffering it endures due to being physically dependent is objectless, for the baby is unaware that the drug can make it feel better. Addiction does not happen in a flash, like lightning, with a single dose of a powerful drug. Of the millions of people who experiment with hard drugs and booze, the vast majority do not become addicted, after all. Addiction sprouts and grows over time in the sunlight and soil of certain conditions—genetic, personal, cultural.

The essential condition is a body, with a brain and a spinal column—that is, a central nervous system. In the brain, just behind the bottom of the eyes, is a cluster of cells called the nucleus accumbens—one cluster in each hemisphere— discovered in 1954 by James Olds and Peter Milner. When they stimulated this part of rats' brains with an electrode, Olds and Milner found that the rats would push a lever as many as two thousand times per hour in order to get another buzz from the electrode, ignoring food, sex, and sleep, in some instances unto death. It was the era of *The Man with the Golden Arm*, of heroin addicts such as William Burroughs, Charlie Parker, and Billie Holiday. That there must be a connection between addiction and the nucleus accumbens was plain, but it was another twenty years before the key presence was identified: the neurotransmitter dopamine, which was established by Roy Wise.

Wise believed he had discovered the "pleasure chemical," the neurobiological essence or substrate of bliss, but within a few years this broad and broadly reported claim was overturned (only to linger in popular culture). Certain dopamine neurons fire in response to distress and punishment, for instance, while others circulate in parts of the brain governing physical movement, something first noted by Oliver Sacks in his work with patients suffering from Parkinson's.

Recent findings suggest that there are at least two basic types of pleasure, which the psychiatrist Donald Klein distinguishes as the "pleasure of the hunt" and the "pleasure of the feast." The pleasure of the hunt is one of drive, confidence, anticipation, focus, foretaste, lust, arousal; the pleasure of the feast is that of satiation, warmth, euphoria, belonging, inclusion, orgasm, attainment. In surf terms, paddling for and catching a wave would be a pleasure of the hunt, versus riding in the barrel then coasting postcoitally onto the shoulder, which would be a pleasure of the feast. In drug terms, cocaine versus heroin, as indeed it was the testimonials of coke addicts and junkies that led Klein to his theory.

As its link to Parkinson's suggests, dopamine produces the pleasure of the hunt—motile and restless, that of wanting rather than the hot-tub gratification of the feast, which is afforded by endorphins and endogenous opioids. In fact, even when their dopamine receptors are blocked, animals can still experience pleasure—the taste of sweetness, for instance; they just lack the motive or motor skills to seek it out.

Yet while it may not be the pleasure chemical, dopamine is an active ingredient in all addictions, whether to stimulants, alcohol, opioids, sex, or surfing. Thought to have evolved as a means of inflecting food and sex with extra appeal, dopamine has a role in learning, habit formation, and memory: a heady experience like riding a wave is tagged by it, singled out and made memorable, desirable, special. Through one channel, the mesolimbic, dopamine brightens the air, quickens the heart and the breath with anticipation, alerts us to the flags under which a pleasurable experience flies: the scent of the ocean and surf wax, summer heat, salt spray blowing back from the crest of a wave. Through another pathway, the nigrostriatal, dopamine creates focus and the will to move toward or away from something.

Shouting at it in dopaminergic language, banging on the negotiating table like Khrushchev with his shoe, hard drugs startle the brain into flooding both the mesolimbic and the nigrostriatal pathways with dopamine, creating excited anticipation and the motivated drive to go after what is being foreshadowed, to hunt it down. Yet for all their diabolic powers of persuasion, drugs soon lose their ability to elicit all-pervading pleasure and/or a sense of potency, as if faltering in their fluency, forgetting key phrases, muttering, falling silent. Why?

To many addicts it's as though what drugs do is take, say, two weeks' or a month's worth of good endogenous neurochemistry and serve it up in a single binge, leaving them with nothing—the "pharmacological Calvinism" syndrome in which one pays for pleasure by dragging through the following days in a listless, semi-depressed state until either this anhedonia passes on its own or the addict is able to do more drugs, recommencing the cycle. In his 2013 memoir, *TC*, two-time world champ Tom Carroll describes his fall into methamphetamine addiction in this vein: "There's a certain amount of life force given to you from the beginning— a number of heartbeats, the amount of energy it takes to give you those heartbeats, what the Chinese would call chi energy. The Hawaiian mana. I really felt I was taking a big chunk of my mana and throwing it down the drain. Literally burning it on the spot—whoosh, gone. Oh my gosh, this is what I'm doing. I won't have any life force left."

That Carroll worried about the depletion of his vitality is understandable given how much he depended on it in his professional career. Though physically small (five-six, 145 pounds), he was a power surfer, famous for levering hacks and gouges on heavy waves. His competitive persona was one of luminous invincibility and toughness, but he had a dreamy, sensitive side that emerged in his photography, which he took up, to the bemusement of his matey fellow competitors, as a way to chronicle and reflect on life and travels. Having risen unerringly through the junior ranks in Australia, Carroll won his two world championships in the 1980s, the era that saw the top surf apparel brands become major companies. In 1988, Carroll signed pro surfing's first million-dollar contract (spread over five years), with Quiksilver. The partying was particularly wild in this period, with the arrival of the tour being the bacchanalic event of the year for the little beach towns on its schedules, and Carroll acquired a taste for "the gack" or "the gear," as Aussies call cocaine. But he was also an early proponent of fitness training and nutritionist-curated diet, alternating between excess and abstinence in a way that reassured him whenever he secretly worried that he was a drug addict in the making.

During his years on the pro tour, when he was in his physical prime and a perennial contender for the world title, and even when he was semiretired but still competing in select events, Carroll was able to party then surf successfully the next day. Or to binge for weeks then abruptly halt and plunge into a lengthy, fearsome training regimen. But the binge-purge binary is itself an addictive rhythm, since it slams the neurochemistry between two poles without establishing a middle or moderate setting. The "off" mode is not truly sobriety, since it depends for its meaning on the existence of the opposite "on" setting. The stout waterman body recovers once the drug misuse ceases, but the puer aeternus mind is keenly aware of the profligate feast of the binge being prepared in the foreseeable future. It's a manic rhythm, a series of cancellations that creates a riven, bina-ristic psyche.

Like all individual sports, competitive surfing can be lonely. The nature of competition is to single out, to sepa-rate. Standing on the beach, each surfer pulls on his or her jersey in a psychological isolation, paddles out alone, wins or loses alone. Carroll also found it solitary, but he was a superstar, marked from his teenage years as special, of world-champion caliber, and in an Australian culture that regarded top surfers as national sports heroes. Carroll met the prime minister, appeared on talk shows. He had his photography and his elfin day-dreaming nature, but he also felt fundamentally at home on the tour among his fellow competitors, contest officials, brand managers.

For Lynne Boyer, whose two world championships came back to back in the late 1970s, life on the tour was harder, in part because of the second-class status of women's surfing—much smaller prize purses, fewer events, little to no media coverage—and in part because Boyer felt obliged to keep her guard up lest her fellow competitors spy a vulnerabil-ity. One weakness was her shyness, which she overcame by drinking and later, after being introduced to it at a contest in Brazil, doing cocaine. Drunk and high, she slept some-times with men, sometimes with women, which confused her and put her further on guard: surfing is a homophobic and, with certain exceptions among the women pros, clos-eted world. Boyer was experimenting, she told herself, but it reinforced the perceived need to maintain a steely front.

Boyer had learned to surf at age eleven, when her family moved from Maryland to Oahu in 1968. Her father was an army physician who retired from the military shortly after

arriving in Hawaii and opened the first oncology wing at
the Queen's Medical Center. Having honed her skills at
various breaks on the South Shore, stamped by Hawaiian
Larry Bertlemann's low-centered, rubbery style, Boyer
worked her way up to the North Shore, where she was often the only girl and later woman in the lineup. It was and
remains a macho, virtually all-male world but one in which
skill and daring are deferred to, and Boyer's athleticism,
talent, and doggedness earned her a place. She was determined to become the Martina Navratilova of surfing and
this ambition was crucial in pushing her past a fear of big
surf following a scary drubbing at fifteen-foot Makaha.
But it was only in contests, with the crowds cleared from
the water at Sunset Beach, that she was able to get the choice
ten- to twelve-foot west-peak waves she dreamed about
charging. Boyer and her rival, Margo Oberg, may as well
have been competing one-on-one in such heats: unac-
customed to Hawaiian surf on this order, the four other
women hovered in or near the channel.

But the stress of competing in the midst of an intensifying addiction to cocaine and alcohol led Boyer to quit
the tour suddenly, mystifying everyone but those closest to
her. She managed to stay clean for ten months without AA
or rehab, living in a condo her mother owned on the North
Shore and working as a sandwich maker at the Ala Moana
Shopping Center. Looking back, Boyer characterizes this
initial sobriety as a "dry drunk"—white-knuckled and
anxiety-ridden. One day after her shift she found herself
buying beer, which led to a three-week binge that ended
when she ran out of booze and coke early one morning.
Her fingernails were bitten down to the quick. She had sat

frozen with paranoia on the couch while watching TV, trying not to think about the holes in the walls through which
people were spying on her. She called her mother and announced that she was ready to do whatever it took to get
better. She remembers the drive that day around the island,
from the North Shore to her parents' house in Kailua, as
the longest, most difficult journey she has ever made.

It was 1981. Boyer spent three months in Hina Mauka
rehabilitation center. Once out, she attended AA meetings
devoutly and worked various low-wage jobs—in the ware-
house of Town & Country Surf Shop, cleaning houses. In
therapy she came to terms with her sexuality.

She also kept surfing through this period, and even competed occasionally, but sobriety and the changes that went
with it had blunted her drive to win—her killer instinct.

Sober and no longer utterly consumed by waves, Boyer
took up fine arts painting, which she had loved in high
school but had dropped out of devotion to the jealous god
of surfing. As a painter, Boyer tried various realist styles,
mastering each with impressive speed, before finding her
niche in impressionist plein air land- and seascapes, which
she was eventually able to sell enough of through galleries
to afford to quit cleaning houses.

In 1994 she met her life partner, Reka. Of the many
surfer addicts I interviewed and researched, Boyer is the
only one who spoke about the problem surfing can present
to relationships. For a long time, Boyer insisted the couple go to surf-break beaches, which are seldom suitable
for the sunbathing and swimming Reka was interested in.
Reka thus became a "surf widow," either left behind at
home or waiting long-sufferingly on shore for her surfer

partner to come in. Eventually Boyer realized that this rigidity on her part was another facet of her addictiveness and began to compromise, agreeing to go to beaches where she could surf—not in the absolute best waves, but surfable— and Reka could happily sunbathe and swim. The couple also spends part of each summer in Reka's home country of Hungary, which Boyer has grown to love—a testament to her evolution from narrow, surf-obsessed pro to painter-surfer Hungaryphile.

Boyer's crisis came while she was competing on tour. For Tom Carroll, it arrived after retirement. Without the structure of the then twenty-five event competition year and the validation of the money that came with it, Carroll was suddenly both adrift and under pressure to support his wife, Lisa, and their two young girls. "My basic reaction was fear," he writes in *TC*.

I'd want to run away, get out and not deal with it, and surfing was great for that. And that filled me with conflict, because I wanted to be a good dad, a good husband, but at some level I was still trying to run. So my idea of a good time was to get a gram or two of cocaine and go on a binge, snort it up. Lisa would get the whole of Tuesday to do a ceramics course, the girls would be taken care of by their grandma and I'd have the day to myself. I was in contact with a guy who had a really good supply at the time, and I'd be jittery over that fact alone. I'd say, Line me up some for next Tuesday, okay? And I'd get relief for about an hour. Maybe. Snort up a couple of lines and feel good and then think, Oh no, now I've gotta do all the rest of this. I was always by myself. No one else had a Tuesday off. I felt really alone in that space. I really felt that loneliness and isolation, and that shame, that really deep-rooted shame that comes with it, to have to face Lisa, the possibility of having to face others. I'd think I could get through it all and come back down so I was ready for Lisa to come home and pick up the girls around 3 or 4 pm. But of course that didn't really work. She'd pick up on what was going on and be really angry. Quite often I would think, Why am I doing this?

THAT SOCIAL ISOLATION and despair are the preconditions of full-blown addiction was first suggested by a study known as "Rat Park," which was conducted in Canada in 1977. Researcher Bruce Alexander was aware of the many experiments in which rat subjects, if allowed to, consumed fatal amounts of heroin or cocaine. As someone who used rats in experiments himself, Alexander wondered whether the typical bareness and solitude of the rats' environments might not play a role in their overdosing. Like people, rats are highly social creatures and sensitive to their living conditions, good or bad. Alexander and his colleagues built a huge (twenty-nine-square-foot) interconnected warren of cages and filled it with straw, woodchip bedding, hiding places, and other rats. There were even forest scenes painted on the walls and plenty of food and water—it was more paradise than park, really. Dispensers of sweetened water laced with morphine were placed around this "rat park." At the same time, other rats were placed alone in typical bare cages, along with food, water, and morphine. The upshot was that rats in paradise showed no interest in the morphine, because they were too busy happily socializing, having sex, and exploring, while the isolated rats took nineteen times as much. Even when both groups had been made dependent on the morphine and taught that taking it would relieve their withdrawal symptoms, the paradise rats were reluctant to use and the solitary rats took eight times as much. The moral, as put by Maia Scalavitz, is that "drugs are powerful primarily when the rest of your life is broken."

Carroll was still able to quit for stretches of as long as two months, which gave him a reassuring sense of self-control. Then he would be triggered by a party or a number appearing on his phone. Though he didn't enjoy drinking alcohol, he came to depend on it as a way to come off a coke binge. He liked to hole up in a small storage room under the house. One day, unable to find him, Lisa realized he must be there under the house and called two of his friends, who arrived and dragged him out. Carroll was so shaken and humiliated by this episode that he attempted to address his addiction in therapy. Because of his special sports-hero stature, he avoided the option of group therapy with other addicts, going instead to someone who'd been recommended. But this therapist was himself using opioids, it emerged, which Carroll took as an excuse to discontinue the sessions. Instead of coming fully out into the open, he became more adept at duplicity.

There is a culture of secrecy in surfing—breaks known only to locals or discovered by small groups of traveling friends. Oaths of silence are sworn and great umbrage is taken at violations and leaks. But this is a fraternal order sort of secrecy. The secrecy of addiction is different. The dealer becomes one's last remaining confidant and confrere. "There was always that weird connection with the dealer," Carroll writes in *TC*. "A conspiracy to escape and make this deal and get high. Often it's done behind the back of someone he's involved with. So it's a very secretive enticing space. Fuck everyone else. The dealer would understand. My ice dealer, in Mona Vale, I remember getting some from him and we were having a pipe together, and he looks at me as he's lighting the pipe, and says, No one understands, do they, Tom? No one understands."

The opposite of addiction, according to Johann Hari, is not sobriety but connection. Aside from the matrix of factors that led them to focus so intensely on surfing to begin with, the common ground between Boyer and Carroll is loneliness. The perceived need on Boyer's part to wall herself off from competitors created the immediate grounds for her addiction. With Carroll, it was everyday life after glory and specialness, the pedestrian yet stressful sphere of being simply a husband, father, and breadwinner. The social confusion that arose with his retirement, of being without his acknowledged status and stature and role, compounded that isolation.

When coke eventually lost its appeal, Carroll turned to Ecstasy, which proved too unpredictable. This period, the mid-1990s through the early 2000s, coincided with a massive expansion of the surfwear brands. As the tide of expanding markets and globalization lifted Quiksilver, Carroll rose, too. The biggest payday came when the sale of his share of a Quiksilver wetsuit franchise netted him just under two million dollars. But financial success, his own and that of his colleagues at Quiksilver, left him feeling oddly untouched, dissatisfied. Money is not glory. The feeling of being high comes closer. Carroll wound up trying amphetamine, which he liked, then crystal meth, which he loved. Meth gave him wonderful clarity and efficiency—ten hours' worth—at first:

> *The ritual of smoking it becomes so addictive. Just like smoking. I'd never tasted smoke like that. It was a totally different kind of smoke. It was just all white. It was like a vapor. The smoke became a heavenly thing. I still like the thought of it. Such a cool smoke, such a beautiful thing. So I'd end up doing more than I'd think because I liked the ritual so much. And all of a sudden you've got more in you than you need, and then you go on for longer. And eventually your body needs more. The spiral becomes quicker, downward, a steeper gradient, falling deeper, steeper and deeper. It's brutal at that point, because you'll have lost so much sleep, and you've got to regain it. I might even sleep for twelve to sixteen hours at a stretch.*

Carroll had convinced his wife that he had gotten clean years earlier, but when he was out of the country in 2006 she discovered a duffel bag full of pipes and lighters and other meth paraphernalia. When she angrily confronted him, he confessed and ultimately, at the urging of a surfer opioid-addict friend who had gotten sober, entered rehab in December 2006.

But just before he did, when he was still vacillating between honesty and the duplicity that had become so reflexive and many-doored, he slipped away. "I remember in the middle of it all, heading up to my office, in secret, and having a pipe—taking a long, deep hit—and it had almost no effect. I couldn't take it. I screamed in frustration: God, help me with this!"

Meanwhile, Carroll's brain had already done its part by preventing him from getting high at this crossroads. For all the talk about its being "hijacked," the brain is not a passive hostage but rather a wily, independent entity that begins resisting the strong-arming claims of drugs almost instantly, with the very first dose. For what the brain has evolved to maintain above all is levelheadedness and clarity of mind in the interest of survival—a state of homeostatic neutrality and readiness. At its most basic level, the brain is thought to be a contrast detector. The homeostatic is rigorously maintained because it is the background against which dramatic phenomena, such as prospects for food, drink, or sex, can be clearly perceived. Anything, any drug or experience that makes one tipsy, high, or drunk—a line of cocaine but also falling in love or violently grieving—will be counteracted by the production of biochemicals that dampen or neutralize the disruption. If a line of coke is the stimulus, opponent processes (as neurologists call these phenomena) begin diminishing its sparkly, eye-widening rush immediately. The next time, and each subsequent time, the dampening effect will be more accurate and widespread, so that while the potency of the stimulus remains objectively the same, the dynamism of the opponent process within the central nervous system is adapting in order to bring the destabilizing, intoxicating effect of the cocaine closer and closer to homeostasis with each dose. In response to the little shots of dopamine pumped up at encounters with typical cues such as straws and mirrors, the crafty, censorious brain produces biochemical countermeasures to countervail the high being predicted and foreshadowed. The brain can be temporarily and partially outfoxed if one takes the drug not late at night in the bathroom of a bar but, for instance, early in the morning in a cornfield—if that's imaginable—but even then the shrewd, dogged brain will soon catch on and catch up.

This phenomenon in which something thrilling and novel gradually becomes familiar and lackluster is itself familiar, of course, and extends to many if not most objects and experiences. A journey to Manhattan on a train the first time is slow and vivid but soon becomes rapid and virtually featureless as a daily commute. The difference when it comes to intoxicants in the context of addiction is one of degree and intensity rather than category or kind. But if the opponent process theory is correct and neurology works according to Newtonian axioms that every action causes an equal and opposite reaction, and what goes up must come down, then the outlook from the addict's perspective is grim: there is no reliable way to keep getting truly high, and there is certainly no way to never come down, which was always my fond wish. Whatever the neurological truth may be, it's the universal experience of addicts that they must take more and more of a given drug in order to approach the unattainable peak of the original pleasure, which is accompanied by the loss of appeal of mundane pleasures, including normally commonplace moods of well-being, curiosity, and human warmth—an altogether bleak state of affairs blandly termed as "tolerance."

There came a time when the uplift and sparkly focus coke magically provided, which simulated inspiration and made writing poetry and academic papers such a pleasure, were replaced by at best relief from ambient depression and anxiety. The crash, which I scarcely noticed in the beginning, came to predominate and I drank heavily to soften its blow, blotting out what little of the original high was still feebly asserting itself.

In the final stage, an initial bump might leave me catatonic, held fast in a kind of metabolic vise. There's a name for this syndrome, it turns out: "sensitization." It's in a way the nightmarish opposite of tolerance: instead of fading in strength and requiring larger doses, the drug's signal is stronger at lower doses yet perversely unpleasant and even painful. The addict's dopaminergic system has become so dysregulated as to cancel out liking or gratification while still creating craving: the addict "wants" the drug more and more while liking it less and less.

What's left to recommend the whole doomed project? Not a thing, less than nothing. So quit! And most do. The average length of heroin addiction is fifteen years. But if many addicts age out, many also die trying to get high in that vanishingly narrow strip of sky left by the low weather of tolerance.

Addiction is not only learned, it's hyperlearned, etched by the extraordinary amounts of dopamine deeply into memory and neurology. This extra dimension assumes the form of "incentive salience," in which otherwise neutral and banal things in the environment around the consumption of a hard drug—an apartment, a bar, a person, a straw, a spoon—become supercharged, talismanic cues. The difference between this sort of stimulus and other associative pairings, such as Proust's madeleine, is categorical: the madeleine catalyzes memory, a reanimation and recovery of the past. Proust remains in his chair gazing ruminatively into space, eventually picking up a pen and beginning to write. The glimpse of a spoon or hypodermic needle or smell of a dive bar sets off cue-induced craving, a wanting that spurs the addict to get the coke or booze being foreshadowed and predicted by the stimulus. The addict becomes tipsy with impulsivity and thus helplessly inclined, even after decades of squeaky-clean abstinence, to hunt down and slam that long-ago sworn-off whiskey or speedball.

Addiction fatally narrows to the source of the drug, which glows with power and magic, the giver of life, sustenance, happiness, freedom. For Carroll, a supercharged cue was his dealer's flashy car. During the years of his active addiction to meth, catching sight of the car somewhere in town would move him to call the dealer up. As part of his recovery program he had of course deleted the dealer's number from his phone. But one day, fresh out of rehab and on the way home from an office job Quiksilver had kindly given him, he encountered the dealer's car in a roundabout. They both stopped.

He said, Haven't seen ya, mate. I could feel myself returning to that same space, thinking, Wow, this is crazy. He said, Where ya been? Everything's good. I said, I don't have your number. I'd better get your number. He said, No worries, let's do it. Yeah, let's do it this afternoon. No worries, I've got it. It's all ready to go.

This was all still in the roundabout. I punched his number into my phone. I hadn't saved it yet. I was looking at myself thinking, Holy shit.

I could feel a surge of adrenalin going through me. When

you're an addict, you start feeling it before you do it, and I was starting to feel that surge, just by looking at the phone number. I said, Okay, I'll give you a call, he said Okay, four o'clock this afternoon, it's on.

But Carroll deleted the number before saving it. He was going to chase the dealer down but called one of his recovery contacts instead.

For me, it was a bodega on Avenue C in Manhattan, festive yellow lightbulbs above the awning. Walking toward it, I was sometimes stopped in my tracks by a leaden foreboding. In warm weather the door was held open by a length of frayed twine. If children were buying candy or an elderly caballero was chatting with the clerk, I drifted down the aisles. Dusty cans of yucca on raw plywood shelves, baby food in glass jars, boxes of Purina Cat Chow. With the coast finally clear I laid a twenty on the counter and the clerk, who knew me by sight, swept it up and produced what looked like a gumball wrapped in yellow paper, which I pocketed, the fragrance of the detergents stacked in the front window lending the transaction a cheap flowery optimism.

It was all so much more foreclosed than I imagined even in my most pessimistic moments, thwarted by the very nature and mission of my central nervous system. Would knowing that have helped me fight free any sooner than I did? I doubt it. Facts are worthless without heart, without blood on the tracks.

It's the soul, split in two, fractured, that must reclaim itself. Where is it? The soul is lost. It's sitting alone in a room in the vast city. The soul wanders the streets listening for its own cry. Nothing else matters.

Now Appeal

One of the central concepts in addiction studies is that of "now appeal," which refers not to the spiritual allure of living in the present moment, as in Ram Dass or Eckhart Tolle, but to the way the siren song of drugs leads an addict to discount or ignore looming negative consequences in favor of getting high—now. Brain science accounts for this impulsivity by pointing to the communication breakdown between the prefrontal cortex and the mesolimbic regions that ensues in addiction: the neurological impairment of the capacity to reflect and choose with deliberation, which constitutes, as we have seen, the basis for the classification of drug addiction as a disease.

In surfing, the premium placed on spontaneity and quick-twitch reflexivity conditions surfers to quiet or mute the cautious prefrontal cortex and heed the limbic and the instinctive. Such surf values arise from the nature of the sport itself, which is to say the protean nature of waves. The face of a wave as field of attention and improvisation in which time slows to the point of becoming spatial and the right decisions are so ineluctably made that the act of choosing vanishes. This is the realm of the zone, of flow—the multivalent, synchronic present. (In the neurological studies of flow states, one thing emerges as consistent: deactivation of the prefrontal cortex.)

The drug high and the flow state are alike in being experientially ahistorical, without precedent, antecedent, without the typical linear narrative of the past threaded through it and running on into the future. From the perspective of flow-state performativity or spiritual experience, to be without the nagging burden of the past, of memories and regrets minor and major, of history as it shades inevitably into self-serving myth and legend, is optimal and desirable. Far too much value and faith are naively accorded to knowledge of history, as if it had really ever been enough to prevent mistakes made in the past from being made again.

But the eternal present of addiction is a zombie version of the flow state. Past and future have fallen away through synaptic disuse and pruning, bringing about measurable changes to the landscape and function of the brain in an exponential feedback loop that leaves the addict shuffling in small, repetitive circles, jerked along by desire cut off from judgment and insight.

Surfers who exploit and in effect celebrate the permutational nature of waves are the ones most beloved and revered, whereas those who impose a kind of template or preordained choreography on the wave may and often do win contests and world championships. The history of surfing teems with contest-winning machines but a relatively small number of inspiring performers—artists, shamans, the surfers with mana.

The most electrifyingly spontaneous surfer in living

memory, combining radically free, creative improvisation
with the athletic ability to execute maneuvers as they occurred to him, was Montgomery Ernest Thomas Kaluhio-
kalani, known by the nickname his grandmother gave him
because of his curly hair, Buttons. The son of an African
American soldier from Texas and a Hawaiian mother, Buttons was born on the North Shore of Oahu but moved to
Waikiki with his mother when he was five (his father had
left by then; Buttons was raised by his mother). He began
surfing a few years later, though not on a surfboard—his
family was just managing to keep enough food on the table: they could hardly afford to buy even a used surfboard.
Buttons filched a plastic lunch tray from school and paddled it out at Walls, his local break. Before he was given his
first guitar, Jimi Hendrix strummed along to blues records
on a broom. Buttons caught waves on the lunch tray, stood
on it, and spun around—an early version of the carving
360s for which he was later renowned. Deprivation seems
to have imprinted him with an alertness to how much could
be done with next to nothing.

On Oahu, the North Shore is "country," slow, soulful,
laid-back, especially in the 1960s and 1970s; Honolulu is
"town," glints of sunlight on the chrome of backed-up traffic, high-rise hotels, hustlers, strip clubs, local kids without
a dime eyeing tourists from around the world on the vacation of a lifetime. In the background, men wearing mirror
shades from "the Company," the crime syndicate made up
during this period of Native Hawaiians, who controlled
prostitution and drugs, illegal gambling, extortion rackets.

One is born with a body of a certain kind, certain gifts
and potentialities, certain limits. The body as vehicle and

condition of possibility. Buttons had the symmetrical mus-
culature of a natural athlete who would have excelled at
most any sport. In his surfing the symmetry finds expression not only in his uncanny balance but in his catlike ability to switch stance mid-maneuver, beginning a reentry
regular-foot then hopping around into goofy-foot along
the coping just before riding back down. It astonished and
delighted, as did the move for which he is best known, the
carving 360, the ultimate form of curvilinear symmetry,
the circle: a button—liquid graffiti.

A surfboard is another kind of body, one born of a moment's design concepts and materials. Innovator Tom Blake
had a superb swimmer's body but lived out his prime in
the 1920s and 1930s, an era of solid wood boards that had
all the maneuverability of coffins. Like a plastic surgeon,
Blake made fundamental alterations to this inheritance—
the fin for stability, the chambering interior for lightness—
but with the exception of his paddleboard designs the
boards he made never matched his gifts. And so he and
his generation stood erect as hood ornaments, playing subtle, teetering games of risk and adjustment as they angled
gracefully to shore.

The great gift to Buttons from his time and place was
the shortboard, specifically the stinger design created by
Hawaiian surf champ Ben Aipa. The stinger's ride is loose,
like a skateboard, especially once the fin is moved up. The
stinger made it possible for Buttons to become Buttons.

The other condition of possibility for Buttons was skateboarding on the hilly roads above Waikiki, which he did as
an alternative to surfing with his friend Mark Liddell and
Larry Bertlemann, their surf mentor. But it was the magi-

cal new polyurethane wheels that underwrote the way they rode, the speed and sudden cornering and pivoting. Their style on land was as it was in the water: distinctively low and rubbery, face bent down near the water's surface or the pavement, one hand then the other stroking the face like a ski pole, the fingertips dragging smoothly or skittering.

Though socially stratified along racial and ethnic lines, Hawaii is far more truly a melting pot than the mainland United States, with intermarriage between Native Hawaiians and members of the groups that have arrived in waves over the decades: Anglo-American, Chinese, Japanese, Portuguese, Filipino, Korean, Tongan, Samoan, Laotian. African Americans came mainly during and following World War II, and not as laborers but as soldiers stationed at military bases, like Buttons's father. Post-overthrow Hawaii never had Jim Crow laws or the binary racism of the mainland, but it has never been some color-blind utopia. The Hawaiian word for people of African descent is *popolo*, which is the dark purple berry of a nightshade plant used for dyeing tapa cloth. While not the equivalent of the n-word (there is no equivalent), *popolo* nonetheless has a derogatory, objectifying force.

As a surfer, Buttons was liminoid, suspended between the straight workaday world and the world of pure play, of eternal youth. As a biracial Black man, he was suspended in another way, between the African American world of the mainland, which he knew primarily through music and TV shows like *Good Times* and *Fat Albert and the Cosby Kids*, and the surrounding Hawaiian community of his mother.

The iconic image of Buttons is of him paddling out on

a brilliantly sunny day, 'fro glistening with droplets of seawater, turning back toward the viewer with a grin to flash the peace sign. Buttons was the unserious sprite of the nascent professional surfing circuit, which suited professional surfing just fine, since it meant that he would not pose a real threat. For Buttons, this position on the happy-go-lucky, slightly mocking outside of the contest world was a safe psychological place to be: If surfing is all about fun and I, Buttons, am the righteous embodiment of that spirit, then there is nothing at stake when I compete. Yet for all the pleasure he took in suggesting as much, Buttons was not some unaware "natural." He later revealed that he had a perfectly good measure of his talent. "If I could turn back the pages I could have been world champion," he said in middle age. The contents of the gift are known to the gifted.

Buttons won two relatively minor professional contests, placed third in several major ones, including the Pipeline Masters of 1981, then disappeared into addiction for twenty-five years.

When he finally reemerged, it was due to a bizarre mass-media intervention: an episode of *Dog the Bounty Hunter*, a reality-TV series starring ex-con Duane "Dog" Chapman—wraparound shades, blond mullet—who, with the help of flinty family members, tracks down and arrests bail bond violators.

The theme of the show is tough-love redemption, and it had a long, successful run, 2005–2012. I watched a few of the episodes set in Hawaii, drawn to it as I had been to *Hawaii Five-O* as a boy: for anything to do with the islands—incidental surf shots, the collision of a violated but still living paradise with pitiless law enforcement. But I missed "The Big Wipeout," as the Buttons episode is called, and learned of its existence only when Buttons had died and his life was being summarized and celebrated. The story is that Buttons had a number of minor drug-possession convictions for which he was given probation instead of jail time, but probation entailed taking periodic drug tests. Unable to quit using heroin and thus aware that he would fail a drug test, Buttons went on the lam, violating both probation and the agreement he had with a bail bondsmen. Enter Dog.

Scripted, melodramatic, false, reality TV can also be raw and accurate. We see the white van Buttons lives out of with a girlfriend in the parking lot of an office building; the expression of shock and shame on his haggard face when he's pulled to his feet after being handcuffed; the bruises or track marks on the girlfriend's bare arms; the blouse hanging from a clothesline strung up inside the van. We see and hear the girlfriend's terrible cry of despair as she learns that Buttons is being arrested, that she won't see him for some time, which she knows may mean never again.

The Buttons who appears in "The Big Wipe-Out" is a gentle, kindhearted man possessed by something that is laying waste to him—illness, addiction, evil spirits, karma, self-loathing, the ill will of jealous gods—call it what you like. He is a captive of a force like Circe. Around and around the island he wanders in a daze, slowly dying. Dog and his family of self-appointed do-gooders, for all their sappy violence and profit motive, are like a squad of mercenary soldiers who stumble upon a hero of legend, bind him, and bear him away.

Off camera, after the producers have turned to the next poor sap on their list of bail jumpers, Buttons undergoes the agony of withdrawal, the worst of which is not physical but psychic—panic, disorientation, self-hatred, loneliness, and abject hopelessness marbled with scheming to somehow get enough heroin to end or suspend the ordeal. When he's strong enough, Buttons begins attending Narcotics Anonymous meetings. He reconciles with his wife, Hiriata, sister of Tahitian surf legend Raimana Van Bastolaer.

Later still, when Buttons has begun to get fit and surf daily, but also when he might have secretly begun to lose interest or belief in this redeemed life; when his very renewed vitality and power might have deluded him into thinking that he's strong enough to dabble, to do just a little or just once—at that moment "The Big Wipe-Out" airs. Well-wishing, prayerful emails, testimonial letters and phone calls from around the surf world reach and move him to remember, to recollect. He's astonished and humbled at the volume, the goodwill. In the consciousness of the thousands of surfers he delighted and inspired, the freedom Buttons embodied has lived on in a kind of independent life, untouched by his fall into addiction. The well-wishers have been infused by his infectious spirit and like donors in the wake of a disaster they come forward to give back the blood of their belief as Buttons hovers in the purgatorial haze of recovery.

Now appeal, the inability to resist the temptation to do drugs in the face of negative consequences, the inability to break the circuit of compulsive misuse, is the result of the silenced mind of active addiction. All life-forms in the field of attention have been drained of color and interest except for the drug, which glows from within from a surcharge of dopamine rerouted by dysregulation. As demonstrated in the research by Volkow and others, the prefrontal cortex, deprived of lifeblood by the neurochemistry of chronic misuse, slips into a kind of stupor or coma. Without its guidance and advice, the limbic region of the brain—site of desire, anticipation, craving, impulse—rubber-stamps the request to inject again.

But as the life of Buttons suggests, addictions fall along a spectrum. There is the familiar tragic mind of addiction, with its stupefied repetition: this is the homeless Buttons in the white van tying off first thing in the morning, beginning to think about how to get the evening fix before the morning hit has fully faded; the maintenance of a numb, detached neutrality, a seeking not so much of pleasure as avoidance of the pain of withdrawal and any clear-eyed assessment of the wreckage, the two overdoses that left him near death, the five children from his first marriage wondering where he was even when he was present, the searing estrangement from Hiriata.

The carving 360 maneuver for which Buttons was famous is a figure of completion or perfection, of an unbroken circuit. It is Buttons's motif or symbol, Buttons's button. Its power derives in part from how neatly it complements his persona as the self-contained or autotelic, capering wise child, the puer aeternus Hawaiiensis. Yet between the performance and the inner actuality there was a gap, a wound, something he could not cope with and which remained. It may have been a very narrow one, just a hairline fracture, but a gap is a gap. It hurts. The pain worsens, calling more attention to itself. Buttons found he could close or heal the gap, make himself whole, first by surfing then by getting high.

After getting sober, Buttons reestablished himself, astonishing the surf cognoscenti with wave riding that arguably surpassed the performances of his prime, along with an iron-man fitness. He opened a surf school and had a second child with Hiriata. In 2012 he was diagnosed with lung cancer, which had taken his mother. In videos made that year, he is emaciated and weak, reflective, somber, though still capable of getting excited as he describes the various sections of a particular wave in Tahiti. He talks about his Hawaiian forebears, who were *paniolos* or Hawaiian cowboys. Further back, his great-great-grandfather was a *kahu*, a protector and priest, in the court of the last Hawaiian king, King Kalakaua. After his parents broke up and his father returned to the mainland, he explored the richness of his mother's ancestry, a genealogical tree on which he saw himself appearing like a leaf. But even in the context of his late-stage cancer, this turn to the past on the part of the ultimate surfer of the present moment and now appeal is striking. It also has a bearing on addiction more broadly.

Growing up, Buttons had seen the rise of the Hawaiian sovereignty movement. The reestablishment of an independent nation or kingdom for people of Native Hawaiian ancestry is the movement's ultimate goal. In the meantime the sovereignty movement sponsors a general revival and celebration of Hawaiian culture and tradition—the preservation and transmission of the Hawaiian language, for instance, which was banned from being taught in schools shortly after the overthrow of Queen Liliuokalani in 1893; the stewardship of the land itself, which entails addressing rampant development and the related desecration of native burial grounds and other sacred spaces, such as the *heiaus* (altars) where Buttons's *kahu* ancestor conducted rituals.

In response to reports of frightfully high suicide rates among First Nations teenagers in Canada, a study was conducted of the roughly two hundred bands or tribal groups residing there. The researchers found that in certain tribal groups the suicide rate was eight hundred times the national average but that in others there were few or even no suicides among the teenagers. Why? The crucial factor turned out to be the presence or absence of cultural transmission. In groups where tribal councils were intact and tribal elders taught the language, history, and culture of the group, teenagers seldom if ever took their own lives. In these intact cultures, the teenagers were given a sense of their meaningful place in the world. The stories, the ways of narrating one's life in terms of the wide and long context of the past, gave the young people a sense of having a future and thus a present. It was the groups where tradition and social continuity had broken down, where the tribal language was no longer known or spoken, where the institutions of justice and culture had faltered or ceased to exist, that had the soaring suicide rates. When interviewed, the teenagers in these tribes had little or nothing to say about themselves, where they had come from, where they saw themselves going, what their futures might hold.

In full-blown addiction, now appeal collapses past and present into a voided present, the site of a slow-motion suicide. I think of Buttons's having to be revived twice after overdosing. He became a zombie state, without past or future, but in the end he overthrew the usurper and reinstated his rightful, original self. His life described the turn for which he was famous: Buttons came full circle, closing the gap.

Bunker

For recovering addict and neuroscientist Judith Grisel, the tragedy of addiction lies in its foreclosure of volition and self-determination: the opposite of addiction is not sobriety, not even connection, as per Johann Hari, but the freedom to choose. Grisel finds expressions like "Drinking is not an option for me" philosophically wrongheaded: authentic abstinence is defined precisely by the existence of the option of drinking, which the recovering addict is deciding, again and again, not to take.

To me, this granular focus on choice is both compelling and a bit foreign. Certainly my daily experience is not one of weighing whether to drink whatever glass of wine happens to pass before me, far less whether to pour one for myself. I have in effect submitted to the ruling handed down long ago by a higher court of myself: no alcohol, no drugs. That is the law of the land and I abide by it more or less thoughtlessly, without relitigation. Then again, there are no drugs coming in across the borders. Like most recovering addicts, I deploy various forms of the Ulysses contract—the metaphor being that of Ulysses's decision, as his ship approached the island of the Sirens, to have his crew lash him to the mast then put wax in their ears, cutting Ulysses down only once they had rowed the ship out of range of the island. Thus, I have no dealers' numbers in my phone or bottles of booze in the house. None of my friends are big drinkers. None do hard drugs. I don't hang out in bars.

But Grisel is right: however automatic it may seem, I'm always in fact choosing, and this ability, this privilege, is precious and definitional of sobriety. What's also true is that it's possible to have too many choices, to be too free for one's own good. The Sirens episode springs from this reality: Ulysses's dark hunger for experience, his desire to know even at the cost of undergoing his own loss of self-mastery, of straining madly at the ropes in an attempt to leap off the ship and swim to captivity and oblivion.

Adolph B. Spreckels III, who went by Bunker, is one of the larger-than-life characters in surfing's gallery of eccentrics and oddballs. Stepson of Clark Gable and great-grandson of sugar baron Claus Spreckels, Bunker was raised in a world of both Hollywood luxury and rigid, traditional expectations. Sent to military school and groomed to become a banker, Bunker was also taught to surf by the Waikiki beachboys at age nine (thanks to Clark Gable) and gradually lost interest in all else. As a teenager, he was either surfing or dealing drugs in the Malibu parking lot in order to have spending money. When the family cut him off, Bunker ran away to Hawaii, where he led a hand-to-mouth existence and became one of the first to ride the lethal rights at Pipeline, alternately kneeling and stand-up surfing on the small boards he helped design.

Art Brewer, the photographer who later saved Andy Irons's life in Indonesia, ran into Bunker on the beach at Pipeline in 1969 not long after he arrived in the islands. They were the same age, Brewer and Bunker—nineteen. Bunker asked Brewer to take portraits of him and his strange red board, which had metal handles set into the rails midway up. Brewer shot two rolls but never heard back from Bunker. When *Modern Photography* offered to put one of the portraits on its cover, Brewer found Bunker's address on Kauai, where Bunker had since moved, and sent him a model release form to sign. Bunker replied with a two-word postcard: NO WAY!

Furious, Brewer answered with a letter excoriating Bunker for being a spoiled rich kid incapable of thinking of anyone but himself. He then informed *Modern Photography* that the model refused to sign the release and tried to forget about the whole thing. Three years later, in 1973, Bunker and a gorgeous girlfriend appeared at the door of Brewer's North Shore rental. Would Brewer like to come to Kauai and take photos of them?

In addition to athleticism, noteworthy surfers have stage presence, a magnetism on a wave that attracts and holds the gaze. Surf photographers are naturally sensitive to this quality, which Bunker had in spades. Despite his lingering resentment, Brewer found himself drawn along.

Since their initial encounter, Bunker had come unexpectedly into a multimillion-dollar inheritance. What does a surfer like this, raised in Hollywood luxury yet expected to lead the conventional acquisitive life of a banker, do with great wealth when it falls into his lap? He buys every surfboard that strikes him as even slightly interesting and before long has the largest private collection in the world. He orders tiny custom hotpants-like trunks from H. Miura and frail solid-gold chains for his biceps. He buys his girl-friend a wardrobe of expensive clothes. He does staggering amounts of drugs and drink. He begins to put on weight, grows sullen and mercurial. He goes on a tour of Europe and South Africa and hires Art Brewer not to lash him to the mast but to chronicle it all—the surfing at Jeffreys Bay, the killing of an antelope on safari, the buck knives, nunchuks, drunken confrontations, dull-eyed hungover mornings.

It was all a kind of joke, according to Bunker, a perfor-mance. He was merely acting out the destiny of a persona he called "the Player." But he had learned martial arts af-ter being badly beaten on Kauai by thugs who thought he might have drugs to steal. The endless array of choices churned up by his inheritance was more than he could navigate. Back in Hawaii following his grand tour, he died of a drug overdose, age twenty-seven.

When Brewer saved Andy Irons's life in Indonesia in 1999, bringing him back from the morphine overdose, Andy was Bunker reincarnated, the puer aeternus born to die of his immortality complex and addiction again and again. Only by then Brewer the witness and chronicler had seen enough and hauled him back to shore. For the moment.

Wavepool Methadone

There's a principle in behavioral psychology called "intermittent reinforcement" that has proven key in understanding how addiction works. B. F. Skinner stumbled on it in 1956 while conducting an experiment about learning that involved rewarding rats with food pellets when they pressed certain levers. Self-sufficient Skinner made his own pellets and when he saw that he was going to run out of them halfway through the experiment, he decided to reward the rats less frequently rather than interrupt it to fix more pellets. Suddenly the rats found that even when they pressed the right lever, they might not be rewarded with a pellet. Skinner was startled to see that instead of decreasing the odds that a rat would press a lever, the uncertainty about whether there would be a reward had the effect of increasing their interest. Not only did the rats press the lever more often when they were unsure about the reward, they persisted in pressing it longer once Skinner had stopped providing the reward, when the show was over.

Subsequent studies have borne out the counterintuitive conclusion of Skinner's experiment: the most effective way to reinforce a behavior in animals is to reward it randomly. Uncertainty of the reward pattern has the effect of making the animal perform the behavior in question more often and reliably, and it will persist in the behavior longer even after the reward has been completely withdrawn.

We human animals are subject to the same principle. One theory concerning intermittent reinforcement is that the brain evolved to be a prediction machine. If we can foresee what's coming, we are better apt to survive. What in the environment allows us to predict? Patterns: tracks, barometric pressure, cloud shapes and coloration, birdsong, rustles in the hedgerow, ripples and swirls in water. Pattern recognition maximizes the effect of energy spent in hunting and gathering. Because it's ultimately a matter of life or death, of bringing down game or not, we are built to be relentless when it comes to deciphering patterns of cause and effect. Hence any sequence that proves to be elusive or enigmatic will exert a tight hold on our attention. Pleasure taken in aesthetic patterns derives from this ancestral preoccupation. Intermittent reinforcement teases and obsesses the prediction-machine brain.

Pattern also plays a strikingly big role in addiction. The uncertainties of the illegal drug world make obtaining and doing drugs there more addictive than in, say, a world in which the same drug, in the same amount, could be purchased legally at a pharmacy. Drugs are rewards, like Skinner's pellets. In the street-drug context, the unpredictability of availability, amount, and purity of the reward create the heightened vigilance and focus of intermittent reinforcement. Big irregular dosing is typical in street drug use and the pattern most conducive to addiction. Yet taking the same drug at the same time of day in the same place—that is regularly and predictably—diminishes its potency and hold over the user. This is the basis for the argument in favor of "maintenance programs" that dispense methadone or Suboxone to treat opioid addiction: if the addict takes the same amount of substitute at the same time of day, before long there is little to no effect, withdrawal is avoided, and therapy and other steps (surfing) toward getting sober can be taken. No longer high yet no longer craving, the addict is emotionally present and thus better apt to address the psychological underpinnings of his or her predicament, without which lasting sobriety may be impossible. (Maintenance treatment seems to work only with opioids, however: alcohol always impairs and stimulants like cocaine are not physically addictive so as to produce withdrawal symptoms.)

In surfing, the very unpredictability of waves as rewards has the effect of intermittent reinforcement and adds a significant layer to its addictiveness. There is no other sport where the playing field as such changes so radically as the surf zone—snowfall on a ski slope is vaguely analogous, if the snow also created the mountain. It's like waiting for the arrival of a migratory species—or for a dealer to show up. Will he ever get here? How good will it be? Strong, weak? Thus the eternal vigilance and hope of the surfer, the difficulty of turning away.

The unpredictability of surf is also why surf competitions often fail as spectacle. Organizers and sponsors give a lot of thought to judging criteria and where to hold contests, but the main reason surfing will never be a major spectator sport is so fundamental that it's passed over in

resigned silence: the ocean as playing field, which introduces variables of a magnitude sports like football and basketball confront only in dreams: the field or court simply
failing to materialize. For even at the best spots on earth,
at the right time of year, weeks can pass without rideable
("contestable") waves coming up. That changeability holds
even moment to moment. If the surf is firing during a heat,
it can suddenly go quiet and a competitor needing to catch
just one more wave of virtually any size and quality in order to win, loses. Better surfers regularly fall to lesser ones
due to this randomness, with the result that when one has
the good fortune to catch a decent wave, the tendency is
to ride that wave carefully, avoiding the exciting but risky
maneuvers in the interest of completing it on one's feet.
The unpredictability of waves thus indirectly encourages
conservatism in competitive surfing, leading to an overall
dullness cracked open by lightning strikes of unpredictable
brilliance: the rare arrival of great surf, and with it a surplus of waves on which to take chances.

In sum, a surfer who wins a contest is overcoming not
only his competitors but the odds that the ocean will send
him or her the best waves, which has so little to do with
skill that it can come to feel like divine favor: the best waves
appear before the surfer upon whom the gods are smiling.
Competitors enter the water and paddle out in order to
prove that they deserve to be respected, revered, celebrated.
But they may well be proven inferior, if not by how they
surf then simply by the failure to get the best waves—the
bad luck of having bad luck.

By far the greatest competitor ever, Kelly Slater is also
the one with by far the most years on tour. His opponents

are now young enough to be his children. Why does he keep at it? As of 2020, it's been a decade since he took his last crown. Slater has a sharp memory for statistics and uses them to motivate himself. He is keenly aware that with each heat loss and failure to claim a tour victory, he dilutes his achievement. Something more powerful than a concern for his legacy compels him to sign on for yet another tour of duty, to book the nth flight to Tahiti or Portugal, where there may or may not be worthy waves, to struggle into a tight colored jersey and probably advance no further than the quarters. In addition to surfing, Slater may well be addicted to competing, which is to say gambling: the supplemental rush of staking his reputation and ego in wagers, in games of chance, which is what surf contests amount to given the randomness of wave patterns. The neurochemical payoff for winning a surf contest, with all the variables and chance weighing against it, is enormous—to win a world championship all the more so. Over time gambling addiction alters neurocircuitry as surely as drugs and with essentially the same synaptic signature.

In 2016 Slater became newly famous for unveiling a wavepool that, more than any single thing he had accomplished, thunderstruck the surf world. Having been around in one form or another since the 1920s, wavepools had only ever generated decidedly weak, lackluster surf. Working for ten years in complete secrecy, Slater collaborated with a team of fluid mechanic specialists, contributing his knowledge of great surf and the bathymetry that produced it, while the scientists designed and tinkered and ran weeks-long, staggeringly complex parallel computer modeling of the cascading consequences of a given decision. The product of this Manhattan Project of surfing is a seven-hundred-yard-long artificial lake—originally built for water-ski training—through which a partially submerged wedge called a hydrofoil is pulled along at speeds of up to eighteen miles per hour by a power train that looks like several freight cars lashed together. The bottom of the lake has been precisely contoured to interact with the surge of displaced water so that together swell and bottom interact to produce a steep, meaty, formally flawless head-high wave that reels off for about fifty seconds and permits slotted tube rides for as long as eleven.

For Slater, whose brilliant technical abilities have been repeatedly stymied by the ocean's fickleness, the Surf Ranch is a kind of technological revenge. With a keystroke, his machine calls up a perfect wave, exorcizing the specters chance and luck that have haunted competitive surfing since its inception in ancient Hawaii. But the revolution may have come too late for Slater, who began working on the wavepool in 2006, when he was still claiming world championships, but who has failed to win any of the competitions held so far at the Surf Ranch. Still, the greater good is not that Slater win but that all competitors be given an equal chance of winning, as on a basketball court or floor exercise mat.

The Surf Ranch has done something else: it has created the equivalent of a designer drug for surf addicts. Slater has always been the most glamorous pro, the surfer invited to celebrity golf events, to hang with rockers and film stars. With the appearance of "Kelly's wave," as it's known, he became overnight a kind of kingpin dealer, a Dr. Feelgood granting entry to a continuous but highly exclusive surf rave. Tickets are not available online. The Surf Ranch is a combination training ground and arena for world tour pros and futuristic playpen for surf legends, industry insiders, and billionaires who rent it out for the day at upwards of fifty thousand dollars.

Hence the fawning nature of the tributes of those who have had a taste and want above all to remain in Slater's favor. "The wave itself is better than any natural wave in the world," gushes four-time world champ Mark Richards. "I never got to see the Beatles, and I never got to see Led Zeppelin, but I got to see the first event [the Freshwater Pro] at the [Surf Ranch] wavepool, and that was just as good." Mr. Pipeline, Gerry Lopez: "Kelly has created the quintessential perfect wave, and to be able to get that over and over and over again is really going to push the envelope of surfing."

In her testimonial, six-time world champ Stephanie Gilmore unwittingly points up a less straightforwardly wonderful aspect of Slater's wave: "The conditions are controlled, you can schedule everything the way you like it." Control and regularity go to the heart of the problem with wavepools: their dullness and predictability. What the machine at Surf Ranch generates is not a true open-ocean wave, which is created by wind energy and sometimes travels thousands of miles before breaking, but a soliton—a singular, one-off wave, a kind of impostor. Before long, this false perfection brings to mind not a "true surfing experience," as Slater hypes it, but a maintenance program for addicts, wherein the scheduled flawlessness of the Surf Ranch waves engender less the high of surfing than the habituation and tolerance of methadone: a way to wean aging surf addicts off the harder stuff, a high-grade, synthetic substitute during flat spells.

Along with chance, the wavepool has removed the magic, species-rich vastness of the ocean wilderness—dolphins bodysurfing alongside surfers at Jeffreys Bay, sharks, rays, ospreys, seagulls, baitfish, seaweed. Awe, in short. "Back, back into time," as Miki Dora says, "where all these animals, all this sea life, all the oysters, shellfish, crustaceans, everything is part of the smell, everything has to come into the focus of the whole experience. If you don't understand that, you're only a pretender. The whole magnificence of riding waves is that living being, that communication between you and the whole existence of reality on this planet."

PART III

Diptych

Early October—windy, cool, clear blue sky. I'm waiting for the 9:09 commuter train into Manhattan. Around me on the platform, people in publishing, media, advertising. I check my work email on my iPhone, then idly click on the bookmarked link of the Manasquan surfcam. I'm not expecting anything of note, but I haven't been paying attention to the forecast in the past few days. The screen fills with surf so dazzlingly good that it has the force of an accusatory summons: *Where are you?*

I stare at the feed, waiting for flaws to emerge that will allow me to go about my day without undue agitation and self-pity. The waves are reeling off so fast that riders are falling behind and being drilled by the lips more often than not—if that qualifies as a defect. The blustery offshore wind is no doubt making the takeoffs blind and sticky. It's also crowded, though it must be just as good at other jetty breaks, most of which will have only a few people out, many none at all.

There's nothing pressing on today's schedule at work. I could unlock my bike in the rack, ride home, grab my board and wetsuit from the garage, and drive to the beach. I could be paddling out in less than two hours. But I don't want to do that. The whipsaw of it is somehow too stressful, vaguely relapse-like. Meanwhile, I keep watching, mesmerized by the beauty of the glittery spinning waves even as the sight of other surfers feasting in my absence is making me unhappy.

When the train pulls in, I click the phone to black out the screen, put it in my pocket, and vow not to check the cam for the rest of the day. It's a matter of not looking, of avoiding torment—a Ulysses contract.

I find a window seat in the first and "quiet" car, feeling calmer as the surfcam-free minutes pass. The northwest wind seems to have strengthened, I notice as we pass a stand of trees. The waves will be even harder to catch. It will be colder, too, though the water at this time of year is still fairly warm, so scratch that. Maybe I should avoid looking at the trees, too.

Entering a station three or four stops down the line, the train slows abruptly. Shouts and screams erupt from outside. I see a woman on the platform frozen in an attitude of horror, eyes wide, one hand to her mouth. No! she screams.

As the train slides gradually to a stop with a long faint squeal, other people come into view on the platform—a woman who glances away with a stricken or sickened expression then others. Anguish and violence hang in the air. I sit listening for gunshots. I'm poised to flee though others in the car seem unfazed and stolid. Finally, a fellow passenger announces in a businesslike way that we're being asked to leave the train.

Everyone rises and files out into the cool windy day and we walk in ragged formation along the platform toward the station. I overhear someone say that a woman jumped in front of the train. On the tracks at the foot of the station steps an EMT crew is pinning up a white sheet. I'm disinclined to look but do anyway, catching sight of a mound-like form on the tracks, strands of frizzy blond hair fluttering in the wind. I glance away and mount the stairs to the station in a crowd.

Someone says she saw the woman leap from the steps of the platform. She was young, a young woman. At first I can't grasp how she could have jumped onto the track when the train was already in the station. I picture her leaping somehow between one of the narrow gaps between the cars, and only later does the actual sequence come into focus: she leaped as the train entered the station and I was seeing people reacting to the sight of her leaping, being struck by the train, then tumbling beneath it.

In the station, police are arriving, an enormous detective wearing a gray suit, more EMT workers. The passengers pass through the doors and out into the entrance area. The collective mood is dazed and rattled. I consider going home then decide against it. Some people are calling Ubers but most wait for the buses that have been called for.

Meanwhile, violence and mutilation hang in the air—of the woman who leaped onto the tracks, the violence done to her body by the iron and steel, by the velocity and bulk of the train. The violence done to the witnesses, and to the witnesses of the witnessing, like me. It seems vaguely blasphemous for there not to be some ceremonial acknowledgment of what we all just experienced, for this to amount merely to a snarl in our commute. We are not equipped to address this rending of the day down the middle like a torn sheet of paper. There is no one among us who might be deputized to say a prayer or in some way mark and transmute the occasion. It's a kind of spiritual bankruptcy in plain view. The body will simply be removed and whatever can't be carried off in plastic bags will be hosed down and away, though bits of gore or stray blond hairs will glow like radioactive embers among the cigarette butts and bottle caps and crushed rock.

I pull out my iPhone and click without thinking on the link to the Manasquan cam, like lighting a cigarette. If anything, the waves are better, the tide fuller and more favorable. I'm hoping to be soothed, but I'm simply seeing that I'm missing something remarkable that won't come again in just this form. That I'm in the wrong place, out of place, in the wrong.

Surfing is the embrace of life with both arms, as paddling is a scooping up of water, the source of life. Suicide is an act of turning fatally away, a species of the isolation and turning away of addiction.

I feel as if I've been shown a split-screen view of the two—surfing on one side, suicide/addiction on the other—not just today but more or less continuously over the course of my life. It's like a diptych I've inherited. It hangs on the wall where I live, this apposition that amounts to a conundrum or riddle I'll be faced with until I can solve it.

Surfing is the world as open, as open ocean. Suicide and addiction are closed forms of seeking release from the torment of the many in the vanishing point of the one—the one of death, the one of being high.

Maybe the answer lies in the form of the conundrum, the division of the diptych into two images. The division that is part of neither—that which cleaves and keeps apart and must be healed, solved, dissolved.

To be all things: waiting for a bus looking at my iPhone, lying dead on the tracks and surfing.

Never not to be surfing.

The Unrecovered

The main social pressure of Western culture is to indi-
viduate. We struggle to distinguish ourselves, to stand
out, to become, in the most recent iteration, some form of
celebrity or personal brand. The long-obvious dark side
of this process is isolation: bowling alone, as the title of
a study on the postwar breakdown of community puts it.
Pride is the hallmark emotion of individuation: I did it my
way. Shame is the underbelly emotion born of the failure to
achieve, to distinguish oneself. Yet everyone in our society
feels some degree of loneliness flavored by the ideology of
the rugged, self-made individual.

In addiction, there is a complex interplay among these
elements—pride, shame, isolation. If connection is the opposite of addiction, isolation is addiction's twin or counter-
part. The suffering born of loneliness leads to drug use,
which leads to shame, which leads to more drug use as a
way to numb the compounded pain. Pride enters the picture as defiance, the sentimental booziness suffusing "My
Way," the moral of which is not the rich variety of the sing-
er's life but that he lived it *his way*.

Along with Jeff Hakman, the other top surfer drug addict in the apparel trade was South African Michael Tomson, who died in 2020, though not of drug use but of throat cancer. Tomson was ranked fifth in the world in 1976 but is remembered for spearheading the so-called backside attack at Pipeline—that is, surfing the left at Pipeline in a regular-foot stance, with one's back to the wave and thus relatively blindly. It was something that had been done before but not with Tomson's programmatic, almost suicidal commitment. Tomson did it his way. He distinguished and branded himself.

The boldness of Tomson's Pipeline surfing carried over to the punky irreverence of Gotcha, which he cofounded in 1978, the same year he emigrated from South Africa to Laguna Beach. With a BA in business from the University of Durban and a deep appreciation of the arts and music, Tomson injected irony and bite into the predominantly understated, conservative realm of beach apparel, having mean-spirited fun with surf snobbery, most famously in a double-page ad campaign in which on the first page there was a black-and-white, starkly Avedon-esque image of a "loser" of some species (dork wearing PARTY MONSTER shirt, abject old guy clutching a paper sack, etc.) with the caption: IF YOU DON'T SURF, DON'T START. On the next page, a color shot of a Gotcha team rider slotted in a barrel or in the midst of some fearsome power carve bearing the caption: IF YOU SURF, NEVER STOP.

The ad gratified the collective ego of the "core" surf demo while inviting nonsurfing aspirants into the fold: if they, too, took pleasure in excluding losers, they might just be hip enough to wear Gotcha. Ignoring the "big is the enemy of cool" lesson of earlier apparel failures such as Hang Ten, Tomson sold to middle-American department stores like JCPenney with one hand and to surf shops with the other. In 1987, a decade after its inception, Gotcha had $75 million in sales, the third best in surf apparel. But that was the apex. Tomson's two-timing approach to markets, along with the bursting of the second surf boom bubble in the early 1990s, saw Gotcha sold to the highest bidder, and the snarkily ironic T-shirts and board shorts were soon available exclusively at Kmart and Sears.

Coke was Tomson's drug. He started using in the 1970s along with virtually everyone else in the surf world and never quit or never for long. It and booze were legible in his puffy, leeringly amused face. Powder cocaine retains an association with wealth and glamour, which is perhaps what inclined Tomson to be nonchalantly candid and unrepentant about his "fondness" for it. He liked to tell the story of having flown to Europe on business only to realize on landing that he had forgotten to pack his stash. He turned on his heel, flew back to LA, retrieved his drugs, and returned to Europe. A thirty-six-hour correction.

There was never a Hakman crossroads for Tomson, never a terrible flameout or come-to-Jesus moment requiring soul-searching and self-reinvention. It's impossible to know precisely why but given how reflexively often Tomson alluded in interviews to his glory days at Pipeline, how important it was to him that he had made a mark, I suspect it was a matter of a particularly stubborn case of pride. The evocation of his backside attack days at Pipe felt good, like a drug hit, but may have been a cover for shame—a way to hide, which is the physical action that shame seems to produce in us, to cover or conceal ourselves. Of the seven or eight basic human emotions, shame is the most painful, along with deep sadness. Shame often elicits anger and aggression, since the implication is that we are being shamed by someone—as indeed we were as children, when the controlling sting of shame is wielded as a means of inculcating how to behave and survive. Shame is bound up in addictive drug use because the sharpness of shame's pain drives one to seek out something to blot it out or make it tolerable—drugs, alcohol. But addictive drug use—stigmatized as character flaw, self-indulgence, personal weakness—leads to a renewal of shame, commencing a cycle that, like waves, either dissipates over time or hits bottom and breaks.

Tomson accrued a criminal record of minor charges gradually increasing in severity and culminating in two felony DUIs and suspicion of cocaine possession (he flicked the vial into highway traffic before it could be found on him). The probation for the felony DUIs led, in 2015, to a surprise inspection of his house, where police found fifty-two grams of coke, scales, and baggies.

Outwardly Tomson treated it all as a nuisance. He complained about the hypocrisy of the surf business class, how widespread the use of cocaine is therein, how Tomson played the role of scapegoat, which permitted surf industry users to feel exempt and superior: I'm no Michael, they would say. Michael takes it too far, Michael has a problem. To which Tomson replied that none of the lot had what it took to lead the backside attack at Pipe and felt better for a moment.

Addiction and surfing, surfing and addiction. Tomson lived by the terminal logic of his best-known slogan: If you don't do drugs, don't start. If you do drugs, never stop.

Gidget's
Intervention

The 1959 movie version of *Gidget*, along with the various sequels and TV-show spinoffs, set off and sustained the biggest wave of interest in surfing the sport has ever seen, with the number of surfers doubling and redoubling three or four times over during the following decade. *Gidget* hauled surfing out of marginal invisibility into the mainstream light of the agora, where it shriveled but did not die, slinking back into liminality toward the end of the 1960s, when the sudden and universal switch to much shorter boards alienated many older surfers and made learning to surf offputtingly difficult except for the committed and obsessive few.

In both the novel (1957) and the movie there is considerable anxiety about this new denizen of youth culture, the "surf bum"—a ne'er-do-well hedonist not unlike another disturbing new type of the period, the drug addict. In the novel, Gidget keeps her infatuation with surfing a secret from her parents for as long as possible, treating the Malibu world like something dangerous and illicit, which surfing still was in 1957. Reduced to begging by their liminoid existence outside the mainstream economy, even for a summer, the teenage surfers snatch up and wolf down the food provided by Gidget like feral dogs, with the clear implication: This is the fate of "bums" of all sorts.

The older and wiser Big Kahuna (Hawaiian for priest or shaman), meanwhile, is the exemplar of someone who has opted out of conventional life, with its compromises and diminishments, and committed himself to surfing as a calling rather than the summer dalliance it is for his teenager acolytes. In the novel, the Big Kahuna is a harmless lady-killer. In the movie, which is far superior and truly grapples with surfing as a social problem, he is a moody Korean War vet, a pilot whose surf-bum life is a reaction to his hatred of the military and regimentation—and by extension, the regimentation and conformism characteristic of postwar existence. This was not Hollywood whimsy. Surfers were often vets during this era, men for whom surfing was both therapy and addiction. As Malibu regular Dave Rochlen says: "We'd spent four or five years in the war and it had all been bad. When the war ended, boom, we were back. It was devotion. Like, 'I'm never going to leave.' We gave ourselves over to it completely." What's shrewd about making the Big Kahuna's character a vet is that the self-sacrifice of soldiers grants them maximum latitude. They have risked their lives for their country, for "freedom." Are you going to say they can't now exercise that freedom—surf for the rest of their days if they want? Yes, replies the movie, because it's time to get back to work and restart the world.

In a pivotal scene, the Big Kahuna's pet mynah bird dies. He buries it on the beach and walks broodingly along the shore. In an attempt to cheer him up, Gidget gushes about how wonderfully self-sufficient he is, how impressive his ability to live life without a goal of any kind, the kind normal people need—before realizing that this makes him seem like a freak or a loser. Gidget then apologizes helplessly, having failed to console and thus prove herself to be a proper woman, which is the rite of passage she is undergoing on the liminal beach.

"What's there to be sorry about?" says the Big Kahuna irritably. "I told you myself I'm a surf bum. There's nothing to be sorry about."

"No, of course not!" Gidget says despondently.

But when the Big Kahuna walks off along the shore, something occurs to her and she calls after him. "Kahuna, could I ask you just one crazy question?"

"Yeah," he says, stopping and turning, as if he's recovered himself somewhat.

Gidget scampers up. "Well, I understand how you said in the war you got sick of all the rules and regulations— well, and about this *dream* you had that when you got loose there would be no more chains, just a free life. Is that right?"

"That's right," he agrees.

"That's what you said *then*."

"That's right," the Big Kahuna says with a shrug, "that's what the man said."

"Only, what if you could go *back* to that time in your life," Gidget proposes. "If something happened and you could *choose all over again*."

"If I could what?" the Big Kahuna asks, as if she's said something unexpected that has touched him somehow.

"If you could *choose*," Gidget says, "*all over again*."

Having turned his back on the world, the Big Kahuna forfeited choice. Now he's a surf bum and an addict: a surf addict living under a kind of spell. With her singsong thought experiment, Gidget has put him under another spell, one in which he can travel back in time to his postwar crossroads and choose again. It's a stealth intervention—also an ironic reversal, since here Gidget is the Big Kahuna shaman—and it works, though we don't see its fruits until the very end of the film, nor is Gidget herself aware of what she has wrought, immersed as she is in the twilight of liminality.

Meanwhile, the Big Kahuna stares at her unreadably, thrusts his hands in the pockets of his jeans, and turns away to gaze at the ocean. One of the ways in which the movie is massively better than the novel is simply by virtue of its medium: in the novel the descriptions of the ocean and surfing are lackluster or wrong about the mechanics of wave riding, but all the movie needs to do is aim its 35-millimeter Technicolor camera at a California point break being stunt-ridden by five or six of the top surfers of the day—Miki Dora, Johnny Fain, and Mike Doyle among them—and magic occurs. But in this shot of the Big Kahuna there are neither waves nor surfers, just flat empty ultramarine water bleeding into the sky that is almost indistinguishable from it: sameness. Surfing is no different from anything else, in the end. Even with Gidget included in the frame, maybe especially so, it's a lonely, slack moment, a portrait of the Big Kahuna in self-doubt and regret on the very threshold of what is supposed to gloriously justify his life's path, the ocean and thus freedom from regimentation. But the structure of the shot also says that he could have the girl/woman, Gidget as any eager girl/woman, but he's turning away from her and the salvation she embodies in a mistaken yearning for some beyond. There is no beyond. The mainstream world of family and work is all there really is. The Big Kahuna's liminality is wrongheaded self-isolation—which is to say this is very much the portrait of an addict.

"Well, I said it was a crazy question!" Gidget blurts finally, snapping the Big Kahuna out of his reverie.

"Cheer up, angel!" he says, turning back to face her with bluff insouciance. "Don't you know that frowning is bad for the face, beautiful? Besides, you're going to the luau!"

But back in his shack, alone, a brooding Big Kahuna fishes a jug of wine out from under his cot and takes a long pull.

In the final scene, Moondoggie and Gidget stroll arm in arm along the shore, where there's no sign of surfing, its sole purpose having been the staging of their union, meanwhile being introduced to the wider world as a sexily charismatic but ultimately safe pastime—the domain of teenagers but *only* of teenagers, with the clear understanding that come the end of summer, the boards get stored in the garages of the tract houses where triumphant young couples live and breed.

The outcome of Gidget's intervention is revealed at the

end as well, when Gidget and Moondoggie discover the Big Kahuna dismantling his beach shack.

"Kahuna, what are you *doing*?" Gidget asks him.

"Closin' up shop!" he says brusquely, tossing a panel of plywood onto the sand. "You know, 'call o' the sea,' 'follow the sun,' and all of that jazz!"

While he and Moondoggie exchange sarcastic remarks about their broken friendship, Gidget notices something on the sand that has fallen out of the Big Kahuna's flight jacket. A close-up shot reveals it to be a laminated ID card:

EMPLOYEE OF TRANS-STATE AIRLINES

Name: Burt Vail

Occupation: Pilot

Start Date: Sept 15, 1959

Stamped Approved.

Signed Richard Woods General Manager

"Jeff!" Gidget says, picking it up and showing it to him. "He's taken a *job*!"

On the ID's other side, which Jeff inspects, is a photo of the Big Kahuna in a collared shirt and blazer.

"Okay, so ya know!" says the Big Kahuna, smiling crookedly. "I can't kid anybody." To Gidget he adds, "You start a guy like me thinkin', it's fatal!"

The Big Kahuna—or should I say at this point Burt Vail—then jauntily tips his commercial pilot's ID at them and walks away carrying a canvas suitcase and no surf-board.

As a replacement therapy for the Big Kahuna's surf ad-diction, becoming a pilot is an elegant solution: flying is as liminal as it gets, but in its commercial form it's also so-cially sanctioned—an approved and remunerative form of living in the clouds.

The First

Even if it occurred in the relatively remote past, in early childhood or youth, most surfers recall their first wave. The thrill of being gathered up and borne along as if by magic triggers a kind of conversion experience, etching itself into memory and neurochemistry. "Suddenly I was like a pelican gliding over the water," remembers *The Endless Summer* costar Mike Hynson. "As that sensation of weightlessness hit, a jolt ran through my entire body. I was experiencing for the first time a natural high. I was hooked."

The use of drug addiction as a metaphor for this bond is almost reflexive among surfers, which makes sense given the sport's history, but the image of addiction is hardly restricted to surfing—it's arguably the dominant trope of our era. As once everything gave you cancer, now everything is addictive—drugs, of course, legal and illegal, with the death toll by overdose averaging around seventy thousand per year in the United States; but also sex, gambling, junk food, exercise, smartphones, Internet porn, and Internet use in general. It's as if any activity might capsize into compulsive misuse. At the same time, it's fashionable to pathologize a pastime for the sake of wit or as a disarming way to boast about an enthusiasm for something dry and demanding. "I'm addicted to Latin grammar." When surfers say that after riding their first waves they were instantly "hooked," as by the fatal barb of heroin, which was its original force, it's tempting to see it as another instance of facetious hyperbole. But as we have seen, in the case of surfing there is actually a neurological basis for the claim and if anything the popularity of the trope obscures that reality as in an echo chamber.

As we have also seen, as powerful and memorable as an initial experience may be, becoming addicted, whether to heroin or surfing, is not instantaneous. It requires coming to know an activity as one that can be reliably turned to for a feeling tone, leaned on, used as a means of coping. Surfing demands obsessive commitment just to gain proficiency—a commitment that is only partially fueled by the intense, adrenalated pleasures of wave riding. The underlying question is, who is sufficiently obsessive to get hooked, and why?

Kelly Slater is only the best known and most accomplished of an exceptionally talented generation, known collectively as the New School or Momentum generation, the latter an allusion to *Momentum*, an influential 1992 video by Taylor Steele in which they appeared. Like Slater, many Momentum surfers came from broken homes dominated by violent alcoholic fathers. Psychic wounds seem to create a craving for the relief of total immersion, which can translate in turn into a capacity and compulsion to lose oneself in the intricacies of mastering a demanding sport or art. At the level of neuroplasticity, trauma may rewire the brain in such a way that intense, immersive activities like surfing act to counterbalance or complement the altered neurobiology.

Domestic turmoil drives the child from the home and into the ocean, where the trials of learning to surf and earning a place in the local lineup, rather than deflect and discourage, offer rewards on a scale and degree of absorption commensurate with the stressors of home life. A new family comes into being, a new child is born. "The only time when I felt good was when I was surfing," Shane Dorian remarks in the documentary *Momentum Generation*. "That's when I had a real sense of purpose. This is who I am. I was that surfer kid, not that bummed-out kid at home." Kelly Slater says simply, "Surfing was my savior."

While in many ways typical in what drove them to surf, the Momentum group was exceptional for a straight-edge rejection of drugs and for the most part even alcohol—as if aware that the very salvational character of surfing comes into being through a susceptibility to addiction that might be kindled at any moment. But it was also a refusal and repudiation of the excesses of the world tour's party culture. The Momentum boys were already surfing faster, along and above the lipline, incorporating aerials. Clean living further set them apart from the previous generation and began a shift in perception of surfers from that of vapid stoner jocks to professional athletes, to the delight of their corporate sponsors. The major surf apparel brands such as Quiksilver had by this point, the early 1990s, attained billion-dollar stature as publicly traded companies, allowing them to offer million-dollar sponsorship deals to these ascendant Momentum surfers, which in turn paid for trainers, coaches, and nutritionists.

The only core member of the Momentum generation to struggle with drug addiction is Benji Weatherley. Lithe as a tall tennis player or swimmer in his competitive prime, Weatherley in his mid-forties is as burly as a bouncer—or his father, who played center for the Oakland Raiders and other NFL teams in the 1970s. It was in flight from this father, a volatile, abusive man, that Weatherley's mother moved the children to the North Shore of Oahu when he was seven.

From a surfer's perspective, Weatherley had an enviable boyhood, riding his first waves at Shores, an inside break of Sunset Beach, then graduating to Sunset proper and the other iconic spots along the "Seven-Mile Miracle," as the North Shore is called. He grew up in a house on the beach at Pipeline, the premier break, which he began surfing at thirteen. "Benji's house" became the gathering place and crash pad for a wide circle of talented, ambitious surf friends, including the core of the Momentum group.

A break where careers can be launched with a single heart-in-throat ride, Pipeline is also statistically the most lethal "wave of consequence" in the world. Weatherley saw between twelve and fifteen people die each winter, not all of them surfers, who generally understood the risks. It was the tourists snatched under by the ferocious rip and the bewildered grief of the survivors that left a mark.

"I remember this one family like it was yesterday," he tells me. "I was fifteen. My mom would always invite them into the house to wait while they searched for the body.

It was dark and the helicopter was looking for the husband—it was always a helicopter and they never, ever found
anyone. The wife kept asking me, 'Do you think they'll
find him? Do you think they'll find him?'"

Weatherley shakes his head and looks away.

"What did you say?"

"I lied and told her I thought they would," he says. His
eyes have teared up. "I was just so sick to my stomach looking at this beautiful young wife. The husband was young.
Their little daughter was crying."

This was the year that he did well enough in amateur
competitions to be offered a sponsorship from Rusty, which
paid him a $750 monthly stipend. Every kid in the water
wanted to be tapped by one of the surf brands. Professional
surfing is to the North Shore as the NBA is to city basketball courts: Many are called but few are chosen. Rec-
ognizing the educational value of traveling the world on
the professional circuit, his mother allowed Benji to quit
attending Kahuku High School, where as one of a handful
of haoles he had been mainly consumed by taking care to
avoid running afoul of the Native Hawaiians.

A few years younger than the others in the Momentum
group, Weatherley looked up to them, but they all stood in
awe of Todd Chesser, an established young pro who coaxed
them into surfing Waimea Bay and outer-reef breaks with
names like Himalayas and Avalanche. Chesser was also
a model of authenticity and groundedness in a world rife
with hype and temptations to surf for the wrong reasons.

In February 1997, when Weatherley and the rest of the
Momentum group were off competing on the world tour,
the inconceivable happened—Chesser drowned, held under

by a twenty-five-foot set at Outside Alligators near Waimea Bay, which breaks half a mile from shore. Ironically he was scheduled to "stunt die" that day on Maui for a scene of *In God's Hands*, a film about big waves, but had stayed on Oahu because the surf was forecast to be giant. The two friends he paddled out with barely survived, one of them puking and sobbing when he reached the surface. They found Chesser floating facedown. By the time they got him to the beach—a terrible, chaotic process due to the size of the surf and the distance of the break from shore—it was too late: Chesser could not be revived.

On the day of the funeral, Weatherley, who had never so much as taken a hit of a joint, decided to give pot a try. "I was the straight one. I'd get mad at my friends if they drank. I was like, 'What are you doing? You're going to ruin it!' I was so driven. But I smoked at Todd's funeral and it just gradually took over my life." He was twenty-one. A decade of booze, Ecstasy, and coke followed. It took two stints in rehab, along with reconciling with his father, to free him of the dependence.

Though Chesser's death devastated everyone in the Momentum crew, each grieved in a private, sealed-off fashion that both expressed and accelerated the breakdown of the group's cohesion and loyalty that was already underway. Theirs was like other packs or gangs that spring up in youth around neighborhood or subcultural identity—jock, stoner, goth, skater, surfer—then eventually and inevitably break up in or on the threshold of adulthood. There is a strong tendency to condescend to gangs, to see them as either laughably adolescent or, in the case of street gangs, alarming and pathological. But gangs are better understood as vestiges of our fundamental social form: the tribe. After all, for most of our collective time on earth, the tribe was the primary and all-important unit, and the individual as we understand it had yet to be born. Something as immemorial as the tribe will persist, sprouting atavistically like new shoots of green on an ancient tree. Tribes were nomadic, moving with the seasonal migration of game, a mobility that enforced communal, egalitarian relations—it was the relatively recent agrarian world that permitted accumulation of wealth and thus social stratification. The values of the tribe are bravery, self-sacrifice, cooperation, sharing, skill in hunting and foraging. And as with other things established over millennia of bioevolutionary time, there is a neurobiological substrate left behind by tribal life. Hits of dopamine and serotonin reward acts of self-sacrificial heroism, sharing, and various forms of hunting and foraging.

Gangs are doomed to break up not because they are products of youthful folly but due to the relentless pressure exerted by the dominant social form: entrepreneurial individualism. Sooner or later, pack members are divided according to slight or great differences in social economic class, employment opportunity, the organizing principle of the nuclear family. Formed when its members were teenagers, the Momentum group was given a lengthy stay of execution through professional surfing, which retreads nomadic tribal life in its hunt for waves and the leisurely waiting around for "contestable" surf to appear or reappear. When Slater won his first world championship in 1992, he was received like a great hunter by the Momentum crew, which took collective pride in it. To celebrate, they put

Slater in a trash can and rolled him down a hill: he was just one of the boys and the boys were all the same. "We were working as a unit," Slater himself says. "Our levels were all rising."

By the time of Chesser's death, professional surfing had gone from being the means by which the tribal cohesion of the Momentum group was given an indefinite stay of execution to being the executioner itself. Now in their mid-twenties, the Momentum tribe had agents, sponsorships of greater or lesser magnitudes with different surf apparel brands, higher or lower competitive rankings. Slater's agent began insisting that Taylor Steele pay a fee for Slater's appearances in Steele's low-budget but hugely influential films. Steele refused in disgust. It was every man for himself and the neurochemical buzz generated by sharing and cooperation was no more. The death of Chesser, their elder and leader, compounded a despair and grief already being felt due to the dissolution of the tribal unity in favor of the lonely management of the self as brand.

Aside from Slater, who won enough crowns to give one to each of them and still have a few left for himself, no other surfer from the Momentum generation plucked down the ultimate, sanctifying plum of a world championship and their competitive careers ended in disappointment and some bitterness. Without soul surfer Chesser to embody a spiritually grounded perspective on fame and officially sanctioned achievement, each surfer slipped into a depression following retirement. Yet only Weatherley got addicted to drugs. Why?

There are always imponderables, factors of set and setting, unseen, unknown, or undetectable stressors. In Weatherley's case, the very intensity of his insistence on straight-edge purity may have masked a latent likelihood of going off the rails. A few years after Chesser's death, when Weatherley had quit the pro tour and had a lot of free time on his hands, he bought a house in Encinitas, where the often mediocre waves invited partying the days away. At that stage he was barely surfing anyway: surfing had taken Chesser—to hell with surfing.

Another factor is all the death Weatherley witnessed during his years growing up in the house at Pipeline and how he interpreted it. Tragic and unbearably sad though it was, the tourists drowned because they were ignorant, the surfers because they were unlucky or not quite good enough. Weatherley himself might have died, too. He didn't put himself above that. "We were pulling into close-outs at Pipe, at Backdoor, on dry reef, two arms behind our backs. You always just wanted to fit in with the craziness, that was the main thing—to see how far you could go without getting really hurt. But I almost died a bunch of times surfing big waves, so I always knew that was a real possibility."

But Chesser was the exception. "Todd was invincible—I believed that. Sure, I could easily not make it, but Todd would always come through. He was just so calm and at home out there when it was huge and out of control." Chesser was essentially unkillable, immortal. This had become a bedrock, quasi-religious conviction. And when the immortal died, Weatherley's belief in meaning, justice, and order also died.

Weatherley was close to Todd's mother, Jeannie Chesser, a surfer who had moved from Florida to Oahu after surviving a car crash in which Todd's father was killed when

Todd was three. She had raised Todd alone. Now, with his drowning, she had lost her son in addition to her husband. Weatherley was scheduled to go to Fiji shortly after the funeral and decided to take Jeannie with him. She cried every night and demanded to know why, why had this happened?

"I told her how God has a bigger plan and all this stuff," Weatherley says, "but in my soul I knew it was just life, how unfair this life is. That the most perfect person could die out of nowhere. And the mom just has to deal with the pain. You can't take it from her. You just have to watch it."

That Chesser died out of nowhere was resonant with earlier experiences of the arbitrary: Weatherley's father's unpredictable violence, the wider uncertainty of his boyhood with money tight at home and school tense with unwelcome. The ocean and surfing had been a source of healing and self-creation, rites of passage in the company of wild-eyed elders on the outer-reef days, primeval vistas appearing on the far side of whitewater mountains, black waves looming like sea monsters. The ocean gave and gave and then took suddenly away, snatched back. The helplessness and despair he felt in Fiji following Chesser's death merged with other, older feelings and beliefs—the anguish and fear experienced by his own mother at the hands of his father when he was a boy, which he witnessed but could not prevent—catalyzing not the addiction but the formation of its grounds, the soil of bewilderment, bereavement, and hopelessness in which addiction germinates and grows.

But let's pause for a moment to recall something perhaps lost in the mist of surf culture and the particulars of Weatherley's psyche, which is that Chesser's death hardly came out of nowhere: the man drowned in twenty-five-foot waves. In addition to being terrifying, huge surf is lethal. The number of big-wave surfers is a tiny, self-selected subset, with generally only the fittest and most adrenaline-addicted even contemplating paddling out once the waves reach the twelve-to-fifteen-foot range, much less twenty-foot and beyond. The number of cars and trucks parked at a big-wave spot on the best day of the year is about the same as at a Little League baseball game.

Still, the death rate of big-wave surfing is surprisingly low compared to other high-risk "extreme" sports. And Chesser, probably in part to stick a pin in the inflated machismo of the big-wave "fraternity," was inclined to demystify the whole thing. "If you know the basics," he wrote in an article published in *Surfer*, "the danger is minimal." Yet two other young, accomplished big-wave surfers died in the years just before Chesser—Mark Foo and Donnie Solomon. For these three, the danger turned out to be maximal, and what good were statistics then?

Foo, Solomon, and Chesser had no drug problems as far as I know, though others in their world certainly did and do. The point is that, whether or not they struggle with drugs, big-wave surfers share an essence with addicts: to overcome the effects of tolerance, of having grown familiar with a certain rush, craving something more powerful, something like their first or best wave, that haunting gold standard, they increase the dose to the very limit of what their bodies can survive. Ross Williams, North Shore local and former world tour pro, is unequivocal about the allure of flirting with death: "Almost dying in big waves, as morbid as it sounds, is one of the things that keeps you coming back—it's a kind of junkie vibe."

Others who survive harrowing, near-death hold-downs are less blasé. In 2010, Shane Dorian fell on a huge wave at Mavericks in Northern California, arguably the most treacherous big wave spot in the world. He lost control at the bottom after hitting a chop and flew head over heels into the frigid water. On the ominous journey back up and over with the main breaking part of the wave, he was able to get his head above water in the cataract-like torrent and draw a quick desperate breath. Then he was driven violently to the bottom, where the water was freezing cold and black. His ears popped painfully from the sudden pressure change and he was rumbled endlessly over rock reef until the wave had finally spent its force and he was able to begin swimming to the surface. By that point he was at the very end of his oxygen; his throat was contracting and spasming. He was within four or five feet of reaching the surface, with daylight streaming down through the layers of foam, when a second wave detonated above his head and he was plunged back into the depths.

Dorian knew how dangerous and worse than useless it was to panic, how it squandered whatever precious reserves he might have left, but he panicked anyway, because it's the nature of panic to occur on the far side of rationality, when all seems lost. "I saw flashes of my son's face looking at me and I was thinking, What the hell am I doing here at the bottom of the ocean in San Francisco when I could be at home right now on a soft longboard in warm water, surfing at Pine Trees [a spot on Kauai]?" He thought about his wife. It was her birthday that day. And he thought: "This is how it happens, right here. This is what Todd Chesser went through, totally out of breath, pinned on the bottom and getting pounded by a huge wave. This is what Donnie Solomon went through. This is truly what big-wave guys experience right before they drown."

Struggling wildly and on the verge of blacking out, Dorian was somehow spun to the surface. Too weak to tread water, he gulped down air in the thick morass of sparkling foam. White spots throbbed in his vision. When a Jet Ski swooped in to pick him up, he could barely raise his arms and drag himself onto the sled. Hauled into a boat by friends who had been anxiously waiting for him to surface, Dorian puked up fluorescent green bile. His lips and face were blue, his thoughts scattered from a concussion sustained in the initial impact of the wipeout or while tumbling along the bottom. "My son!" he muttered when he could finally speak. "My son!"

Dorian was so shaken that he swore off big-wave surfing. He was done, he told people. Let the younger guys have it, the ones without families to consider: Dorian was over it. But as the weeks passed and the symptoms of the concussion cleared up, the old cravings stirred. He wanted to ride big waves again after all, he realized. Not only that, he wanted another go at Mavericks—a redemption session.

Meanwhile, there was his family, the wife and young son who had appeared in his vision on the threshold of death. Somehow Dorian had to improve his chances of survival. He was thinking about it on a flight, idly watching the instructional video of a flight attendant blowing air into a life jacket. Big-wave surfers were already wearing safety vests for extra flotation. What if the vests could inflate? Working with his main sponsor, Billabong, Dorian designed a vest with ballasts that fill with air from a CO_2 cartridge when a toggle is pulled, sending the wiped-out surfer up to the surface as on a rope let down by God. Since their introduction in 2012, no surfer wearing one has drowned. It's a kind of Narcan for big-wave junkies.

Still, safety vests malfunction, leashes snap, Jet Skis fail to ride to the rescue. Surfers drown after being knocked out on impact with the water or reef or board. Sharks attack only rarely but attack they do, maiming and even killing.

Another danger lurks on land, treacherous because unexpected, in the way that descending a mountain after a climb is the time when accidents occur. This peril flows from the impetus to keep the buzz and exaltation going, or to generate a substitute buzz in the absence of surf, when surfing is impossible—the problem of downtime, in other words, when workaday earthly existence displaces the all-immersive, moment-to-moment demands of surfing.

Big-wave surfing is simply surfing writ large rather than some categorically distinct, superior form—truer and greater than the rest, as many big-wave surfers take sly, faux-modest pleasure in suggesting. But the neurochemical rush of riding and surviving huge surf is indeed enormous, commensurate with the risks run and the sheer physics of surfing at that scale. Hence it's among big-wave surfers that the problem of downtime is clearest. A stout South African charger hints at it when he says, "Here in Cape Town we get maybe one or two big swells a year. And that's when you sort of push the family off. And even afterward, when the adrenaline kicks in, after the surf. The comedown."

Peter Mel, a champion big-wave surfer from Santa Cruz, California, taller than most at six-two, dark-haired with handsome square features, is interesting in part because he seems so unlikely a drug addict. Since retiring from competition he has worked as a webcast commentator on the World Surf League and his affect is one of probity and caution—tight-lipped, measured, a little dour.

To his credit Mel has been forthright about his slide into addiction, which he, too, links to the problem of downtime: "The best part of it all is actually when a big-wave session's all said and done. Sometimes the buzz lasts a day, sometimes a few days. But you want to keep it going. Maybe a drink to keep up the buzz. Then other drugs, too, unfortunately."

For Mel it was cocaine that changed the rules of the game, erasing the borders separating the après-surf party from the rest of the week. The long gloom-inducing Northern Californian off-season—cold, hyper-bright spring with bad winds, followed by flat foggy summer—had always been hard. Coke was simply a way to keep his spirits up, he told himself, but in fact it was just another version of the old story, an interlocking, self-reinforcing syndrome tailored to surfing: the big-wave addiction left him depressed in the absence of huge surf, and the coke lifted him out of the dumps but fleetingly and at the cost of his honesty and self-respect.

Mel had climbed the pecking order at Steamer Lane as part of a tight clique of talented teenagers with nicknames like Flea, Barney, Skindog, and Ratboy, who intimidated outsiders and traveled as a mouthy, sneering pack, brawling with others on the surf contest road. They were the best all-around surfers Santa Cruz had ever forged, with solid sponsorship deals and fame that reached beyond the surf media to glossies like *Vanity Fair*. When Mel turned to coke,

he and the Santa Cruz crew were in their early thirties. As
with the Momentum group, the tribal unity established in
their teens and sustained into their twenties had been riven
by the same divisions along minor but invidious differences
in ranking, contracts, and competition results—the unde-
niable and unremitting pressure to stand alone and naked
in the cold light of market valuation. And what comes with
the breaking apart of tribal belonging? A certain neurochemical depletion and cessation—no more dopamine hits
from running with the pack, of fighting together; no longer
the oxytocin born of sharing and cooperation.

This was in the early aughts, when methamphetamine
swept into town. Struggling to lose the booze weight, Mel
gave meth a try and fell in love. Before long it was his thinness people noticed. Because he was up on meth most of
the time, he was also high during surf sessions at Mavericks, which allowed him to shake off wipeouts that might
otherwise have left him badly rattled, even frightened him
away from big waves entirely—Shane Dorian wipeouts.
This power to soothe and steady, to detach, is a secondary
but important characteristic of meth, which works by stimulating a huge production mainly of dopamine, but also
norepinephrine and serotonin, while also preventing their
reabsorption, so that they pool and linger among the syn-
apses, which fire and fire and fire—the dopamine jacking
the user up with amphetamine's famous energy and focus,
the serotonin and norepinephrine relaxing and steadying,
giving the overall high a purring, silky tone. All is vividly
lit up and fascinating and all is also well. Until the lights
begin to flicker.

Mel wound up cutting the cable wires to his house to

silence voices talking to him through the TV converter box, confessed his addiction to his family, and got clean in rehab in 2006.

His friend and archrival Darryl "Flea" Virostko, face like a Russian boxer's, kept using for another two years, pounding a half gallon of vodka mixed with Gatorade every day and sparking bowls of meth as he tooled around town in a dying Toyota Tundra. Flea first surfed Mavericks high on half a tab of acid and later, like Mel, on meth. They both yearned for the validation of a sanctioned contest victory there, to be crowned the official king of this newly discovered world-class big wave, but Flea wanted it a little more desperately, was more reckless and willing to die: he won three consecutive Mavericks Invitationals, pipping Mel in the finals of each, along with Kelly Slater in the third. The wipeouts Flea survived along the way, leaps and trapdoor drops from the tops of five-story waves, are as iconic as anything else he did. And as if he could operate in no other mode, he was climbing a cliff after a sleepless night or two of tweaky partying when he looked up on hearing his name, blacked out, and fell, performing a languid backflip during the sixty-foot plummet and bouncing to a halt on the twisted remains of a steel pier.

As with a wipeout that would have caused anyone else to quit, the bottom of the cliff was not Flea's bottom. Medevacked to a hospital, he recovered from a badly broken arm and lacerated face, and kept partying for a few more weeks before agreeing to enter rehab after his family staged an intervention. He arrived at the rehab facility in Monterey with a near-fatal blood alcohol level and cigarettes packed with weed. But he did get sober there and has since founded FleaHab, a rehab center in Santa Cruz that incorporates surfing into the recovery process. As with awareness of the danger of big-wave surfing, sobriety can get harder rather than easier. "Getting clean and all that shit is good but it gets harder as I go," Flea remarked in the early days of his sobriety. "There's wreckage."

The meth thread, once pulled, ravels all through the Santa Cruz surf scene, up and down the coast, around the world. Anthony Ruffo, a decade older than Mel and Flea and the first fully sponsored pro from Santa Cruz, was initially addicted to what they called "cover acid": the dazzling rush and ego-glorification of having an action photo of oneself appear on the cover of a surf magazine. Ruffo began using meth in his mid-thirties but only descended into full-blown addiction when he was dropped by his main sponsor a few years later. He had expected to go on being a sponsored pro forever; what was he supposed to do now? Heavy use of meth led to dealing it, which led to working with the Norteños, a Latino gang that, when Ruffo was ripped off at gunpoint, was planning to murder the thieves in question but the chance never emerged. Busted in 2005 for possession with intent to sell, Ruffo got off with probation; busted again in 2010, he was looking at five years in prison but got clean via a program built around special breathing techniques and ultimately did only nine months in the county jail. Now he works with various surf therapy programs—for addicts, for at-risk youth, for military veterans suffering from PTSD.

There was burly Pete Davi from Monterey, who earned the nickname Pipeline Pete during his years charging on

189 THE FIRST —

the North Shore, then drowned on a huge day at Ghost Trees in 2007 with meth in his bloodstream.

There was sweet, born-again Chris Brown from Santa Barbara, who walked away from the professional contest circuit to work as a sea urchin and abalone diver, meanwhile reinventing himself as a big-wave charger. He fell from a cliff in 2019, age forty-eight, and drowned after striking his head, with "acute methamphetamine intoxication" listed among the coroner's findings.

There was the somber redhead I met in the Zippers lineup in Cabo San Lucas, a tile worker from Santa Cruz. Having recently gone off meth, he had gained so much weight that his board no longer floated him properly. He sat submerged to his collarbone, listless and depressed. I saw a relapse in his future.

People who become surfers in childhood or adolescence often want to do nothing else but surf. It's truly a form of intoxication, of possession. High school is merely tolerated and surfers do not typically get four-year college degrees. In the short term, this hardly matters, since during their teens and twenties and thirties, the years of their physical prime, they happily take jobs that leave them time to surf and take surf trips—in restaurants and bars and hotels, surf shops or surfboard factories, construction trades, lawn maintenance, lifeguarding, commercial fishing. But "down the track," as they say in Australia, with their thirties behind them and their bodies no longer indefatigable or injury-free, surfers might understandably weary of bartending or tile work, wish they had a better education, more options. In demographic terms, the vast majority are "non-college

whites" in a globalized labor market shot through with uncertainty, upheaval, and a steeply rising number of "deaths
of despair" (suicide, alcoholism, overdoses) among white
working-class men over the past twenty-five years.

To say of their first wave, as so many surfers reflexively
do, that it seized them like a drug testifies to the addictive power of surfing but perhaps more importantly helps
justify and make sense of a whole formative period during
which choice was always present but may as well have been
absent, because there was nothing as compelling to choose
instead. That one is always choosing among forms of captivity, passions that bind. The first wave, the one that creates the surfer, is bondage. What characterizes the origin
stories of surfers is *amor fati*, the love of the captive for the
captor.

Surf Therapy

Like finally reading a classic, I surf Malibu for the first time, squired there one day in April 2019 by former pro and writer Jamie Brisick. It's a warm sunny afternoon, the desert scrub on the hillsides in yellow and blue bloom. We arrive in the famous parking lot empty-handed: I didn't bring a board from New Jersey and Jamie's Point Dume rental burned to the ground in the Woolsey fire—dishes, books, clothes, photo albums, keepsakes, surfboards—all gone. Jamie is betting we'll be able to borrow boards and the first person we meet is JP Pereat, an old friend, who lends us soft tops from his van as though it had been arranged in advance.

As we pull on our wetsuits (I did pack a wetsuit), I ask JP about the spare soft tops. He's middle-aged and trim, with close-cropped hair and an unguarded, intense manner I instantly like. Growing up, he helped take care of his autistic nephew, JP tells me. When he introduced the boy to surfing, it was so dramatically beneficial that JP began getting other on-spectrum kids into the water. Now he runs surf therapy foundations called the Mighty Under Dogs and Pelican Ocean Therapy, and is involved with another, A Walk on Water.

The ethos of surfing falls along a spectrum. On one end, the sturdy self-reliance and heroism of the waterman and waterwoman—lifeguard and big-wave legend Eddie Aikau, for instance, who died in 1978 while paddling for help when the voyaging canoe *Hōkūleʻa* was foundering in heavy seas; and elegant surf champion Rell Sunn, Hawaii's first full-time woman lifeguard and an ambassador of traditional Hawaiian culture.

On the opposite end, the selfishness and narcissism of the puer aeternus, the arrested child-god Peter Pan. Malibu's own Miki "Da Cat" Dora, sneering style master and inveterate scammer, springs to mind. In the film *Surfers*, Dora sets forth the Peter Pan credo:

> *My whole life is this escape, my whole life is this wave: I drop into it, set the whole thing up, pull off a bottom turn, pull up into it, and shoot for my life, going for broke, man! And behind me, all the shit goes over my back: the screaming parents, teachers, police, priests, politicians, kneeboarders, windsurfers—they're all going over the falls headfirst into the reef—headfirst into the fucking reef— bwa! And I shoot for my life and when it starts to close out, I pull off the bottom and out through the back. And I pick up another one and do the same goddamn thing.*

Dora was in his fifties when he laid down that riff. As adolescent as it is, it moves me. I feel in it the pulse of surfing's original appeal, its thrilling embrace of the untamed and contempt for the fear-based social order on shore, including all forms of dutiful goodness and volunteerism. For most of surfing's modern existence, the puer aeternus has been ascendant. Aside from a fitful environmentalism and the role it has played in the evolution of water safety, surfing has been either unapologetically selfish or sheepishly selfish. But the puer aeternus/puella aeterna is not an exclusively or even mainly negative formation, since he or she exemplifies a kind of purity and clarity. This is why Dora, for all his faults (and they are many), remains an icon: the thoroughgoingness of his hedonism gets to the heart of the whole project of surfing in its modern incarnation—that simply to follow one's pleasure in the ocean, without regard for whether it's producing anything more than personal fulfillment, amounts to a rousing critique of the acquisitive, work-obsessed social order.

But since the turn of the millennium, the waterman/ waterwoman constellation has been on the rise. There has been a renewed push on the part of surfers to save surf spots from ruination by industry and development and the oceans from plastic and trash pollution. Surfer-led beach cleanups have become standard. Programs to make clean drinking water available in remote parts of surf-destination countries such as Indonesia have sprung up.

Closer to home, many well-known professional surfers have lent their name and time to organizations devoted to surf therapy. The first of these was Surfers Healing, established in 1996 by Israel Paskowitz and his wife, Danielle, following the discovery—as with JP and his nephew—of the remarkably soothing, integrating effect of surfing on their autistic son, Isaiah. According to the International Surf Therapy Organization, which was established in 2017, there are now at least thirty-one such foundations. Surf therapy has been shown to be effective in the treatment not only of on-spectrum disorders but of a range of ailments, syndromes, and conditions: cystic fibrosis, PTSD, drug addiction, special needs, and depression. The results, which tend to overlap across these cohorts, are compelling but not yet well understood. In the case of on-spectrum children, it's theorized that the ocean is both visually stimulating and reassuringly enveloping. It also seems to be that learning the new motor skills required for surfing reshapes abnormal frontal brain structure. For war veterans suffering from PTSD, surfing brings them into the present, pushing traumatic thoughts and memories to the periphery while rewiring neurocircuitry. For addiction, surf therapy works much as it does for veterans who have PTSD.

Surf therapy is in turn part of a broader movement of outdoor therapies whose simple but groundbreaking shift is not only up off the chair or couch of the traditional therapeutic office but out of the office altogether. Supported by data showing that being physically active in stimulus-rich natural settings makes people more open psychologically, a slew of hyphenated approaches have been born: wilderness, adventure, nature-based, equine- and animal-assisted, garden, and horticultural.

As we cross the threshold from the parking lot to the sand, Jamie whispers the name of a '70s surf star and nods in the direction of a sixty-something man with a bleary, alcoholic vibe in a baseball cap, shorts, and tube socks pulled up high above sneakers. He walks, bent forward, along the base of the wall toward a mound of possessions. I'm quietly shocked, though I know next to nothing about the man aside from sequences of him in top films of the 1970s, magazine photos, perhaps an interview I read long ago as a boy. He is forever astounded, that boy in me, to find that talent and daring don't end in honor and comfort. That surfing is unable to save its children, or teach them. I think of a Pipeline prodigy last seen working at a Denny's in Orange County. Of the surf star who at the peak of his fame in the early 1970s had a fabulous foppish rock-star wardrobe and chauffeur for his Rolls but now drives an Uber. It's not waiting tables at Denny's or driving a cab as such that stings and disorients; it's that the glory of their wave-riding youth did not translate into something commensurate afterward. That the blue-green caverns they stood in like gods did not somehow amount to anything more lasting than photos or a film sequence. The greatest things surfers do and achieve mean nothing, do not in a certain crucial way exist beyond the surf zone, which may be the exact price, to the penny, of liminal life.

We walk down the beach, Jamie, JP, and I. The sun has slipped behind clouds and the water appears dark on approach then clear up close. We pick our way across the rocks in the low-tide shallows, begin paddling. Always the feeling of return, like a small bell ringing. The notion that I'm entering one of the most famous, storied surf spots in the world falls away as I respond to a stream of small but urgent claims on my attention. There are no plaques memorializing legendary rides, no statues of Dora or Gidget. The ocean is ahistorical and speaks in one tense only, the present continuous.

There are more women and women of color in the lineup than I'm used to seeing in New Jersey or elsewhere, nearly fifty percent. An open-faced, approachable bunch. They are Malibu now. I am, too, for the moment.

The old-timers say the wave doesn't connect all the way across as it used to, before a dredging operation in the 1980s. But it seems pretty perfect to me. If you catch the right one in the right spot, which I eventually do, the ride is long and subtly demanding, the lipline rising like a rope being hauled from the dark blue water until the beach suddenly appears and you either kick out or ride it to the last drop and stumble onto the sand.

A FEW DAYS later, I rendezvous with writer Michael Scott Moore at his house in Redondo Beach and we set off for Camp Pendleton to volunteer with the Jimmy Miller Memorial Foundation. Miller was a beloved surfer-lifeguard who introduced many youngsters to the ocean and surfing through the Junior Lifeguard Program in the South Bay area of Los Angeles. In his early thirties, when he began to suffer from depression, he found that surfing was the best therapy for regulating his moods. But while recovering from an injury that kept him out of the water, he took his own life. He was thirty-five. The foundation offers ocean and surf therapy to marines suffering from PTSD in the Wounded Warrior Battalion-West.

Early morning traffic on the 405 is heavy in both directions, with fog or smog rising miasmatically from the south intensifying the multilane dreariness. Michael Scott Moore first came to my attention in 2010 through his wonderful book *Sweetness and Blood*, which is about the spread of surfing from Hawaii and California around the world.

Then in early 2012 I read a brief shocking report: he had
been taken hostage by pirates in Somalia while there doing
research for a book. He was freed after having been a captive for more than two and a half years. I met him in New
York, shortly after his book about the experience, *The Desert and the Sea*, was published in 2018.

The traffic eventually thins out and we end up arriving early at the Camp Pendleton visitors' center. Mike has
volunteered here three or four times and knows the drill.
He and Jimmy Miller were classmates at Mira Costa High
School and he feels a personal connection to Jimmy's
family—and to the military, which was ready to rescue him
had the order come down, though it never did. When he
returned from Somalia he was experiencing symptoms of
PTSD himself—hypervigilance, anxiety in the presence of
strangers—and he credits surfing with helping his body remember how to heal itself, which helped heal his spirit.

After a kind of DMV experience getting approved to
enter the base, we join a small group of other volunteers—
friendly surfers of various ages, women and men—and climb
into minivans and follow a marine from the Wounded Warrior Battalion through the main gate, onto the base and
down along a road to a parking lot where the sky acquires a
sudden coastal openness. There are large stucco bathhouses
and modest single-story military housing units with stu-
pendous views of the Pacific. At the sight and smell of the
ocean I feel the ageless excitement and forget for a moment
why I'm here. The blue-gray waves are three to four foot
and rather crumbly and shapeless in a light onshore breeze
but perfectly adequate for the occasion. Without waves,
this long-ago-scheduled event would have to be postponed.

Milling around on the beach are fifteen or so veterans, mostly young men but a few young women. The vibe is serious, impassive, perhaps a bit leery. PTSD is an "invisible wound." Its symptoms are isolation and avoidance of preferred activities; hypervigilance or a constant state of fight-or-flight; and flashbacks and nightmares in which the trauma is reexperienced. Many people suffering from it develop addictions, and the current model of addiction as one that grows out of trauma puts drug addiction and PTSD on a continuum.

The leader of the event is bearded, charismatic Kevin Sousa, who looks like a hipster football coach. I know from emailing with him that he's a rock musician with an MA in counseling psychology who overcame his drug and alcohol addiction in part by training for and completing the Catalina Classic, a thirty-two-mile paddleboard race.

Sousa has everyone sit in a large circle and talks about Jimmy Miller and his legacy. Like Michael Scott Moore, many of the volunteers knew Jimmy and nod and smile at Sousa's recollections. Sousa has in his hand the paddleboard-shaped teak trophy Miller received for finishing the race in the top ten. Thirty-two miles. It's completely abstract to me until I think of it in terms of the distance from Montclair to Manhattan, which is seventeen miles. So it would be like paddling to Manhattan and then turning around and paddling back to Montclair. My God.

Sousa proposes that each of us say something on the subject of asking for help, using the trophy as a talking stick. I'm so preoccupied by thinking about what I plan to say when my turn finally comes that I can't recall anyone else's responses, though most are brief and a few marines opt to say nothing at all and simply pass the trophy, which disturbs me faintly. When the trophy reaches me, I confess to having trouble asking for help, which I connect to the everyone-for-themselves ethos of surfing and how this also feeds into my dislike of lifeguards, which elicits laughter though also a frown and disapproving shake of the head from one of the younger volunteers, a professional lifeguard who is the chief surf instructor.

The marines break into groups and are shown how to paddle and pop to their feet on soft tops lying on the sand. I sip a cup of coffee provided by a volunteer and make mental notes of the vivid way the young lifeguard volunteer is introducing surf technique. Meanwhile, the surf has improved—it's bigger now and breaking better.

Not far from here, on the northwestern edge of Camp Pendleton, is a famous cobblestone point break called Trestles. Spared the usual chockablock residential development all around it, that area of the base is still pristine wetlands and estuaries, with mountain lions and foxes living in the foothills. Until 1971 Trestles was off-limits to beachgoers, but the wave was so good that surfers sneaked in at the risk of fines, board seizures, and even arrest. There's an iconic photo from 1969 of a tight-lipped flat-topped marine in fatigues striding up the beach carrying a confiscated surfboard, the very embodiment of killjoy militarism. This was the year President Nixon bought a house on a bluff overlooking Trestles, and whenever he was in residence at what came to be called the Western White House, security measures bristled, with warning shots fired over the heads of trespassing surfers. But as San Diego surfer Chuck Hasley quipped, "Trestles was one beachhead the marines could never hold." That the Corps is now, fifty years later, welcoming surfers onto its base in order to help heal its soldiers is both a rich historical irony and a testament to the military's ability to evolve.

The photo of the board-confiscating marine was taken by Ron Stoner, whose signature images are among the greatest in the canon. You would often see them in poster form on the walls of bedrooms: a lone surfer knee-paddles toward a green pitching sheet-glass wave that looms across the middle ground, pelicans in the blue air above—the stirring perfection of it, the sense of amplitude, of space and light as alive—the fact that such glory exists on earth. In a way it didn't exist: Stoner had access to the exclusive, prelapsarian precincts of Hollister Ranch, from which the teeming hordes of regular-joe surfers were strictly banned. Stoner was the lyric poet of the 1960s, the Beach Boys of surf photography.

Like many surfers of the time, the shy, socially awkward Stoner, whose nickname was Clark Kent, tried and liked LSD—liked it to a fault. When the only girlfriend he'd ever had broke up with him near the end of 1968, Stoner went on a kind of acid bender, appearing at the *Surfer* magazine offices speaking in memorized Bible verses. Worried about what might happen if Stoner drove home in his car in such a state, the magazine's founder and editor in chief, John Severson, took him to a psychiatric hospital, where Stoner was diagnosed with schizophrenia, institutionalized, and given electroshock treatments. He recovered enough to resume taking photographs for *Surfer* but was institutionalized a second time when he carried a giant wooden cross he had built through his neighborhood in Dana Point wearing a white robe.

Television and print media at the time promoted the claim that LSD was the cause of psychosis in people like Stoner and Jackie Eberle, Jeff Hakman's friend, but given the absence of such outcomes when LSD was administered in clinical or therapeutic settings the current thinking is that unsupervised LSD trips amounted to traumas triggering latent mental illness that would have been set off by any number of deeply jarring experiences.

Following the crucifix episode, there were no more outbursts from Stoner, but he also quit taking photographs. He moved to Maui at the beginning of the 1970s, supported by checks from his family. He would be seen sitting on the breakwater at Lahaina in the morning and then again in the early evening, as if he hadn't moved all day. Back in Pasadena for the holidays, Stoner barely spoke. In 1977 his mother's weekly letters to Maui were returned. No one in his family ever saw Stoner again. He was listed as a missing person in 1978 and declared dead in 1994.

It's noteworthy that just as surfing, once regarded as dangerously subversive, has emerged as a therapeutic tool, so have LSD and psychedelics such as psilocybin, the active ingredient in magic mushrooms. The two rebirths have an unobvious connection: the return to nature. In the case of surfing, the connection is clear: many of the benefits offered by surf therapy derive simply from safe, supported immersion in ocean wilderness. With LSD, as Michael Pollan points out in *How to Change Your Mind*, the return to nature lies in the drug's origins in the fungus ergot, which was used traditionally by midwives to stimulate labor and to stanch bleeding postpartum. Albert Hofmann, the Swiss chemist who invented LSD in 1938 while in the employ of Sandoz Laboratories, had systematically synthesized the alkaloid compounds in ergot in the hope of creating a marketable drug, concluding in the end that there was none. Then, five years later, in 1943, Hofmann felt drawn to reconsider the twenty-fifth molecule in the series. While resynthesizing it, he absorbed a tiny amount and had the world's first LSD trip—a mild and largely pleasant one, which famously came on as he was riding his bike home from the lab. Intrigued, he took what he thought was a safely small dose a few days later. This second trip was horrific: objects assumed grotesque, menacing forms, Hofmann became convinced that a demon had taken possession of him, then that he had simply gone insane, and finally that he was in the process of dying. He saw himself from above lying dead on the couch. But as he came down, he took a walk in the garden of his house, where he had a lyrical, mystical experience: "Everything glistened and sparkled in a fresh light. The world was as if newly created."

In 1947, Sandoz introduced LSD as a psychiatric panacea and it was used with remarkable success in the 1950s and 1960s to treat alcohol and tobacco addiction. Having had a transformative experience on the psychedelic plant belladonna, Alcoholics Anonymous founder Bill W. suggested that LSD be incorporated into the AA program (it was not).

But once LSD was distributed beyond the academic research community via apostles like Timothy Leary, bad things happened to enough people using it unsupervised—as with Ron Stoner—that its reputation was blighted. It was made illegal in 1966 and lost its legitimacy as a therapeutic tool and subject of research. Richard Nixon was convinced that LSD was the root cause of the antiwar movement and of hippies in general. In previous generations, young men had obediently gone to war when they were told to. What was the difference with Vietnam? LSD.

In the past decade, partly due to studies showing that SSRI drugs such as Prozac work little better than place-bos, LSD has begun to be rehabilitated—used in microdose (subhallucinogenic) amounts to treat depression and mood disorders, for instance. Psilocybin has been the subject of clinical trials at New York University and Johns Hopkins University to address existential crises confronting peo-ple on the threshold of dying of terminal diseases. The initial findings are very promising. Studies are currently underway exploring the use of psilocybin as a treatment for depression. The takeaway of the therapeutic use of psy-chedelics is that the strength of the experience is an index of the degree of the benefits: the more powerful experi-ences result in the most dramatic and long-lasting positive changes in patients.

I ESCORT THE first group of veterans into and through the shorebreak. Instantly, the overcast, dispiriting weather ceases to matter. The land-based self dies a little on entering the ocean—it is diminished, forced to acknowledge its in-expertise and minority, to submit to oceanic laws. Everyone benefits from this humbling process, but for people suf-fering from PTSD or addiction, the weakening of the grip on the familiar managerial ego is especially good. In a view that has emerged from psychedelic therapeutic treatments, the ego is a kind of god of the crossroads who patrols the border between self and other, conscious and unconscious, subject and object. Trauma threatens the ego's very existence, causing it to become hypervigilant, playing and replaying the tape of the trauma that menaced it in panicky attempts to master the threat. The ego-patrolled border takes the form of a trench, dug by repetition, which prevents the cross-border influx of new thoughts and experiences. Isolation ensues and intensifies. Without fresh perspectives from the outside, the sense of being trapped, under siege, seems insurmountable. This is where several disorders flow together: PTSD, addiction, disabling fear of death on the part of the terminally ill. While the softening of the ego in surf therapy is mild compared to the obliteration that can occur on psychedelics, it allows new thoughts and emotions to slip past the border.

SOUSA HAS ASSIGNED me the role of helping marines gather themselves after a wipeout or at the end of a ride and I swim out to where the whitewater is fizzling out in a trough. It's like waiting at the bottom of a driveway when someone is learning to ride a bike.

Meanwhile, the experienced volunteers paddle out alongside the marines on their own soft tops, sitting side by side in the lineup and speaking quietly. The contrapuntal rhythm of surfing lends itself to therapy: paddling and wave riding elicits a flow state, which then acts as a cushion for painful memories and emotions that may arise, which can be addressed during the calm intervals between waves. Surfing amounts to an inversion of PTSD, promoting immersion rather than isolation—immersion in the group in this case, being part of a team or unit, and immersion in the ocean itself. There is heightened awareness, as on a combat mission, but it's punctuated not by the terror of a firefight but the arrival of a wave to ride, and thus a pleasurable adrenaline rush instead of a frightening one. Above all, surfing requires focus in the present: it's nigh impossible to be held in the clutches of a thought-pattern loop when being pummeled by a wave. To be blindsided by whitewater as you surface, or tumbled and spun underwater during a wipeout, flushes the psyche clear. One feels shaken in a good way, wrung out, reset.

As happens often with beach breaks, the waves are tricky to line up and time, and there are many false starts and instant wipeouts. A large dense flock of black-and-white seabirds wheels through the surf zone crying out in an eerie metallic voice. I'm beginning to wonder whether anyone's going to get a legitimate ride when a burly, athletic marine springs to his feet and shoots along in a wide stance all the way to the end of the wave while everyone hoots and shouts. As I help him get properly situated on the board and swim alongside him as he paddles back out, he's beaming and exhilarated, and I can feel a kind of electricity coming off him. This breakthrough seems to be infectious: others begin catching and riding waves. My throat grows hoarse from shouting and hooting.

Once all the marines have had sessions, they gather on the beach for debriefing and discussion. The surf instructors, meanwhile, stay behind to catch a few waves. There's been an uptick in the swell size and simply making the drops of set waves is challenging on the soft-top longboards we're all riding, enforcing a playful, lighthearted spirit. And it occurs to me how amusingly typical it is of surfers, even the Good Samaritan sort, to seize the moment while there are waves to ride, forgetting about the beach and its tribulations.

When I mention this to Kevin Sousa at the office of his therapy practice in Hermosa Beach, he tells me a little sternly that when the veterans came in and the instructors were out blithely catching waves, one of the beach volunteers called Sousa over. A veteran needed help. What's up? Sousa asked the vet in question.

He was sitting on the sand. He was just a little emotional, he told Sousa: he'd been planning to kill himself but decided to give this surf therapy thing a chance.

He felt better now, the vet said. He would be back.

IN JULY, A Walk on Water comes to Spring Lake, New Jersey, for a two-day event. JP will be leading the surf instructors. He had a typically strange surfer childhood, I find out chatting with him on the phone. After his Argentinian father left his Peruvian mother when JP was four, he was raised in LA by his mother, who spoke no English, and sent to a Seventh-day Adventist boarding school in Ventura County when he was thirteen. Later he spent time in Hawaii, then came the long and important caretaking of his autistic nephew, William, which led to working with AWOW and the founding of Pelican Ocean Therapy.

Registering to volunteer on the AWOW website, I notice

a stipulation that first-time volunteers should sign up as a (mere) "beach volunteer." But having taught surfing off and on since I was a teenager, and knowing JP a bit, I put myself down as a "surf instructor." If this is a test of my willingness to humbly serve in whatever capacity, I fail it. I seem to need to be a cool kid.

Spring Lake is more suburban and sanitized than funkier Manasquan just to the south. The morning is hot and sunny, but the light, as a photographer will later complain to me, is "wonky," with a sort of atmospheric blur from passing clouds and salt spray in the onshore wind.

Walking along the boardwalk, I scan the beach for signs of the event. I'm expecting something on the order of the humble foldout card tables from my amateur contest days but eventually realize that the cream-colored Fashion Week sort of tents my eye has been passing over are AWOW. JOHN PAUL MITCHELL SYSTEMS, a sponsor, is printed along the flaps of the main one. There are stacks of wetsuits of various sizes, Katin T-shirts, and baseball caps bearing the stylishly designed AWOW crest. I give my name to a friendly, yoga-fashionable woman with a clipboard. When she can't find it on the list of surf instructors, I drop JP's name.

"Oh, okay!" she says, glancing around. "I don't see him now, but talk to JP—he'll get you set up."

AWOW people are greeting families, finding the right-sized wetsuits and lifejackets for the special-needs kids, some of whom, taking in the surf, look as though they may be having second thoughts. The boards to be used are ten SUPs lying on the sand. I can understand why—the boatlike extra flotation and length—but I've never ridden a wave on one, only paddled around in a harbor. Seeing the families up close, I grow a little apprehensive at the prospect of being entrusted with a child, catching a wave, and hauling her to her feet by the back of the lifejacket as I've seen it done in videos on the AWOW website. The physical demand of that move alone, not to speak of the responsibility, is causing me to have second thoughts of my own now that I'm on the verge of trying it for the first time in front of what will be a crowd of anxiously watching parents.

I spot a jet-lagged JP near the main tent and go over to greet him. As he's being drawn away to attend to something, he introduces me to a friendly bearded man in an AWOW baseball cap and windbreaker who turns out to be the event director, Sean Swentek. Sean is under the impression that I'm writing an article for a magazine, so I ask him a journalist question: Tell me a story about the effect of surf therapy on a child with special needs.

"Not long after AWOW started up in 2012," he says half over his shoulder as he walks around inspecting things, "a four-year-old boy named Jacob came to an event. He was autistic/nonverbal and really resistant. It took a lot of cajoling just to get him into a wetsuit and in the water. There were violent outbursts and screaming—he was pretty miserable! But his parents really wanted him to try this, so the instructor finally got him on a board and paddled him out past the lineup and just sat with him for about forty minutes, just hanging out. And then they actually rode a few waves and when they came in the instructor looked completely wrung out and I went up to him and said, 'How'd that go?' And the parents came up, too. And the instructor said that as soon as they caught a wave, it was great. Jacob was, like, 'More!' and 'Surf!' and 'Water!' And the parents were, like, 'What are you talking about? He's never spoken in his life—he's *nonverbal*!' And the instructor was, like, 'Well, he started talking out in the ocean.'

"And Jacob has been surfing with us for the past seven or so years," Swentek concludes, "and if he saw you today, he'd come up and say 'Hi!' and tell you all about how much he loves surfing."

"Beach volunteers!" someone shouts. "Grab a blue rash guard and go with Jim!"

Jim waves his arms over his head.

"Surf instructors! Grab a black rash guard and go with JP!"

When I join the small group of surf instructors, JP asks me whether I've ever used a SUP board with a special-needs kid. With the eyes of the surf instructors turned toward me, a possible impostor in their midst, I admit that I have not.

"Well, maybe work with the beach volunteer crew for the morning," JP tells me, "and you can try surf instruction in the afternoon."

Crestfallen though also relieved, I trade in my cool black rash guard for a pedestrian blue one and join the beach volunteers.

"You look like a strong swimmer," the group leader tells me as if intuiting my neediness. "Let's have you patrol the jetty to be sure no one gets close to the rocks."

Flattered, I fetch my fins from my backpack, walk to the jetty, and swim out along the rocks. Maybe I can be a hero after all.

The warm-up act is a white Labrador retriever named

Haole Boy who rides a few waves into the shorepound in the stiff-legged, stoic manner of surfing dogs, which amuses the kids and casts a lighthearted spell over the proceedings. Still, there are last-second anxiety attacks and tears to be soothed away by the beach volunteers before the first group of children can entrust themselves to the surf instructors. The raw fear at the liminal edge of the world flickers vicariously back to life as I watch them confront and overcome it or be distracted long enough to be paddled out a short distance from shore, where they surrender to the experience and fall quiet.

Soon a surf instructor has caught a wave, hopped to his feet, and pulled his child up to a standing position by the back of the life jacket—they are surfing! I had blandly watched video clips of this on the foundation's website, but it's altogether astonishing and moving to see in person. And the shout of joy and stoke that goes up from the beach! And how the ecstatically beaming child knows the cheers are for him or her! It's the purest distillation of surf stoke I think I've ever witnessed. Some of the rides are longish and entertaining, including rollercoastering on the part of a younger surf instructor I single out to admire and envy, and stylish or goofy dismounts by the kids.

Once it's clear that the jetty is safely distant from the action and there's no current pulling toward it, I rejoin the beach volunteers and wind up making a specialty of plucking children from the shorepound at the end of their sessions, which is an increasingly chaotic affair as a high tide fills in. With a small child in one arm, I'm reaching for a loose SUP when it's flung upward by whitewater and cracks me in the jaw like an uppercut.

"Oh my God, are you okay?"

"I'm fine!" I'm actually unsteady on my feet and my jaw will be sore later.

"You're bleeding!"

I touch my chin—my fingertips are bloody. But looking at my reflection in someone's mirrored shades, I see it's just a scrape.

Working with these kids returns me to a period of my own childhood I haven't thought of in some time. My maternal grandmother opened the first school in Selma for special-needs children and when I visited in the summer she would take me there to hang out. I remember the large bright room where we played music with percussion instruments while sitting in a circle on the floor. We made art, we walked to the public pool and went swimming. There was a girl with Down syndrome named Belinda whose face and personality I recall clearly. The atmosphere was one of matter-of-fact acceptance and happiness. Everything was all right—as in surfing, come to think of it—complete.

As midday passes into afternoon following a brief lunch break, I'm strangely tireless and upbeat. I assume this has to do with being at the beach, but I may be feeling a bit of what's called the helper's high: feel-good neurochemistry elicited by giving unto others—dopamine, oxytocin, serotonin. The bioevolutionary account of this reward is that when we act altruistically, we ensure the survival of the group, thus the euphoria of volunteerism.

Addicts in recovery are often urged to lend a hand in some way—to make the coffee at recovery meetings, tell the story of their addiction to other addicts, fold up the chairs at the end. To begin in humble ways to reverse or counteract the self-centricity of addiction, establish new patterns. There is the age-old ethical basis for this behavior, but it also simply feels good, perhaps for the reasons posited by bioevolutionary theory, though surely that's not the whole story. The dysregulation of neurochemistry that occurs in long-term addiction, the "hijacking" of the reward circuitry, may be most effectively undone by helping others, which would be fitting. But it's noteworthy that the helper's high is not exactly a liberation of the hijacked reward circuitry, only a *different* channeling of the neurobiology. As Larissa MacFarquhar shows in *Strangers Drowning* (2015), a study of extreme volunteerism, even altruism can look a lot like addiction. The blind pharmacist in the brain asks no questions before doling out the good drugs.

I never do surf with the kids. With the arrival of a crew from Montauk, there's a surplus of experienced young volunteers, including East Coast pros Balaram Stack and Sam Hammer, standing around like idle ranch hands. But being on the threshold of surfing hour after hour without ever actually doing it begins to take a toll on my sanity. Having placed a child on Sam Hammer's board, I go on guiding the board outward with one hand, past the point where Hammer needs any help from me, if he ever did. It's absurd, but I can't bring myself to relinquish the board, I want to be on it myself—to go surfing! Hammer finally turns and snaps, "I got it!"

At day's end there's an awards ceremony. The families and the volunteers gather around a table bearing trophies and Sean Swentek calls the names of the children one by one. As the parents and the AWOW photographer record everything, each child comes forward with a swagger or shyly or impassively and accepts a trophy testifying to their bravery and accomplishment. "We don't have school pictures," a mother says of these surf therapy days. "He's not in school long enough to have them taken. So our house has five-year-old surfer Ben. Six-year-old surfer Ben. Seven-year-old surfer Ben. Every year, our house is littered with pictures of him surfing and the success that he's had. This is the Christmas concert that I never get to go to; this is the Little League practice that we'll never make; this is the Mother's Day crafts that were never made in school and sent home. This is everything that every parent gets to experience daily that I don't get to experience."

I'm sun-roasted and exhausted now. JP and the AWOW team are, too, but they have a fundraiser to attend tonight, and then tomorrow another full program with a different roster of families. Then back to LA. I understand what keeps them going: the purity of the stoke—to witness as if at its birth the brilliance and blessing of surfing.

Looking Back

Walking away, surfers pause to look back at the waves. That's the rule. The one who exits the water, strides up the beach and out of view of the ocean without at least a furtive glance over the shoulder is the exception. What's it like now, seen from afar? The same, better, worse? Am I missing anything, did I leave too soon? Nah, it was time to go—it's worse now, dropping, not breaking as well. Or simply to look, with no particular purpose beyond a dazed reflex to bathe the eyes in narcotizing sunlight on ocean, perhaps see someone get a good wave or wipe out.

Surfing is a materialism, after all. There must be waves to ride, and if there are waves unridden within reach, like lines of drugs undone, it nags and tugs at one: Look back, come back, do me. Looking back is just another reflexive attempt to extend the session, to keep the high alive, in the way of all addicts. For there is never enough, nor is satiation the point or the goal—surfing is the goal, just as life is the goal for the living.

According to ancient legend, Orpheus, son of Apollo and the muse Calliope, fell in love with a beautiful mortal

woman named Eurydice. They were enormously happy together, but not long after their marriage, Eurydice was bitten by a snake and died. Grieving in song with a lyre given
to him by his father, Orpheus moved the whole world to
tears, even the gods. He was granted permission to descend
into the underworld to see his beloved one last time, and
there Orpheus sang so touchingly that Hades agreed to let
Eurydice return with him to the world—on one condition:
that Orpheus not look back as he and Eurydice make their
way back together.

But it was a long, unnervingly silent ascent and just before reaching the surface, with the light beginning to stream
in from above, Orpheus, fearing he had been tricked, turned
to be sure Eurydice was really there—and instantly she fell
back into the underworld and was forever lost to him.

Why was he forbidden to look back to begin with? As
a test of his faith. Orpheus was being asked to believe in
the presence of his beloved, and in the reality of her resurrection, without any proof that she was actually with him,
that they were going to emerge finally into the sunlight together.

When he turned to see with his own eyes, he revealed
that he was unprepared for her return. For the upper realm
he was about to enter with Eurydice was not the mundane
world he had left but one necessarily transformed—a world
of the heart and love, in which the presence of his beloved
is not subject to the laws of optics, nor is there any need
to look and see, for lover and beloved are one. It's the only
way. Everything else ends in heartbreak and death. But Orpheus was not ready.

In the end, the identity of "surfer" or "poet," like any

and all identities, like personhood itself, must be discarded. What Orpheus reveals when he looks back is not only his lack of faith in love, but how looking itself is an expression of the estrangement of duality, of being a separate person looking at another separate person—even the beloved, even the ocean.

But let's not inadvertently glorify the past. Orpheus died of a drug overdose at twenty-seven. He was just another rocker poet addict, compulsive, vulnerable to now appeal: he turned and consumed Eurydice with his eyes, drank her in. He knew better, but resurrection has never been a matter of knowledge, only of faith and love.

Acknowledgments

My heartfelt thanks to Kirby Kim, who challenged me to go beyond my original concept for this book and waited patiently for what eventually emerged, which he then put into the hands of all the right people. Thanks also to Eloy Bleifuss of Janklow & Nesbit Associates.

My deep gratitude to Karen Rinaldi for her friendship, generosity, and wise, bighearted editing. There is no one else in the world better suited for this project, and how blessed I was to be able to write with her encouragement and guidance on two topics that touch me so profoundly. And to surf with my editor!

For his belief, kindness, and conversation, my thanks to Joel Rose.

A thousand thanks to Jamie Brisick, who offered invaluable encouragement and support and instantly put me in touch with anyone in the surf world I cared to contact.

Thanks to the surfers who spoke with me about often

painful experiences and memories, especially Benji Weatherley, Lynne Boyer, Tom Carroll, Anthony Ruffo, and Van Curaza. Thanks also to Ben Marcus, Mark Cunningham, Tony Caramanico, Art Brewer, and Jeff Crawford.

Thanks to Michael Scott Moore, who offered valuable feedback about early versions of the book.

For his stunningly perfect cover image, thanks to surf photographer Brian Bielmann.

Thanks to Nancy Miller and Kevin Sousa of the Jimmy Miller Memorial Foundation. And to JP Pereat of A Walk on Water.

Thanks to the generous Matt Warshaw of the *The Encyclopedia of Surfing*, a resource I turned to daily.

I'm also indebted to recovered addicts and researchers Maia Scalavitz, Marc Lewis, and Judith Grisel, who took the time to clarify key points about the neurology of addiction.

Thanks to the stellar team at HarperWave: Haley Swanson, Yelena Nesbit, Sophia Lauriello, Rebecca Raskin, Laura Cole, Elisa Cohen, and Andrew Jacobs.

My gratitude to Kai Bird at the Leon Levy Center for Biography for his generosity of spirit and writerly solidarity. And to Shelby White of the Leon Levy Foundation.

Belated thanks to Patricia Martin, the first teacher to illuminate the beauty and necessity of devotion to grammar, word choice, and logic.

J. Anderson was there for me through some extremely rough times, and for his loyalty and love I am forever thankful.

Unending gratitude for my mother, Pali Summerlin—inspiration, spiritual teacher, giver of iPhone satsangs.

For Len and Carol Ellman I am deeply grateful for their love and support.

And to Teo and Gemma, for simply being who they are.

Finally my deep and undying gratitude to Juliana Ellman, my heart.

About the Author

THAD ZIOLKOWSKI is the author of the memoir *On a Wave*, which was a finalist for the PEN/Martha Albrand Award in 2003, and *Wichita*, a novel. His essays and reviews have appeared in the *New York Times, Slate, Bookforum, Artforum, Travel & Leisure,* and *Interview* magazine. He has a PhD in English literature from Yale University and is the recipient of a Guggenheim Fellowship. He is the associate director of the Leon Levy Center for Biography at the Graduate Center, City University of New York.